The Gulf War

LANDMARK PRESIDENTIAL DECISIONS

Series Editor
Michael Nelson

Advisory Board
Meena Bose
Brendan J. Doherty
Richard J. Ellis
Lori Cox Han
James Oakes
Barbara A. Perry
Andrew Rudalevige

The Gulf War

George H. W. Bush and American Grand Strategy in the Post–Cold War Era

Spencer D. Bakich

University Press of Kansas

© 2024 by the University Press of Kansas
All rights reserved

Published by the University Press of Kansas (Lawrence, Kansas 66045), which was organized by the Kansas Board of Regents and is operated and funded by Emporia State University, Fort Hays State University, Kansas State University, Pittsburg State University, the University of Kansas, and Wichita State University.

Library of Congress Cataloging-in-Publication Data

Names: Bakich, Spencer D., author.
Title: The Gulf War : George H. W. Bush and the American grand strategy in the post–Cold War era / Spencer D. Bakich.
Other titles: George H. W. Bush and the American grand strategy in the post–Cold War era
Description: Lawrence, Kansas : University Press of Kansas, 2024 | Series: Landmark presidential decisions | Includes bibliographical references.
Identifiers: LCCN 2023049700 (print) | LCCN 2023049701 (ebook)
  ISBN 9780700636877 (cloth)
  ISBN 9780700636884 (paperback)
  ISBN 9780700636891 (ebook)
Subjects: LCSH: Bush, George, 1924-2018—Military leadership. | Persian Gulf War, 1991—Causes. | Persian Gulf War, 1991—Diplomatic history. | Operation Desert Shield, 1990-1991. | United States—Foreign relations—1989-1993. | United States—Politics and government—1989-1993.
Classification: LCC DS79.719 .B35 2024 (print) | LCC DS79.719 (ebook) | DDC 956.7044/22—dc23/eng/20240326
LC record available at https://lccn.loc.gov/2023049700.
LC ebook record available at https://lccn.loc.gov/2023049701.

British Library Cataloguing-in-Publication Data is available.

For my inspiring father, Peter Bakich.

CONTENTS

Foreword by Meena Bose   ix

Acknowledgments   xiii

Introduction   1

Chapter 1. George Bush: President and Strategist   10

Chapter 2. The New World Order Grand Strategy, 1989–1990   31

Chapter 3. Operation Desert Shield and the Decision for War   55

Chapter 4. Operation Desert Storm   82

Chapter 5. War and Statecraft in the Post–Cold War Era   105

Notes   117

Bibliographic Essay   135

Index   141

FOREWORD

The George H. W. Bush presidency witnessed significant changes in the international world order. In 1989, Bush's first year in office, China brutally suppressed protests against the government in Tiananmen Square; reform movements came to power in Eastern Europe, ending decades-long communist regimes; and the Berlin Wall came down, with images of crowds demolishing segments of the barrier and streaming through border crossings powerfully signaling the end of the forty-plus-year Cold War. Over the next three years, the apartheid regime of racial segregation in South Africa ended and anti-apartheid activist Nelson Mandela became the first democratically elected president, after being imprisoned for twenty-seven years; democratic governments were elected in El Salvador and Nicaragua; and the Cold War officially ended with the dissolution of the Soviet Union into independent republics in December 1991.

President Bush was uniquely prepared to address the global changes that took place during his four years in office. After serving in the US House of Representatives for two terms, he was appointed US ambassador to the United Nations (UN) in the Nixon administration, making multiple contacts within US diplomatic circles as well as foreign missions to the UN. Following two years as ambassador, Bush served as head of the Republican National Committee and then became US envoy to China in the Ford administration for two years, after which he became director of the Central Intelligence Agency. In 1980, Bush competed for the Republican presidential nomination and though he lost the nomination to Ronald Reagan, he joined the ticket as Reagan's vice-presidential candidate. For the eight years of the Reagan presidency, Vice President Bush represented the United States on multiple visits abroad and was part of the president's decision-making team in foreign affairs. When he became president in 1989, Bush had close to two decades of experience working with diplomats and elected officials worldwide.

This book examines how President Bush navigated the world's transition from the Cold War to the post–Cold War era. International affairs expert Spencer D. Bakich analyzes the Bush administration's development of a new doctrine to replace the "containment" policy that had governed US foreign policy for more than forty years. Bush had navigated Cold War politics throughout his political career, and he saw up close how US policy changed during the Reagan presidency from a strong anti-Soviet stance in Reagan's first term to four historic US-Soviet summit meetings in the second term. Becoming president immediately after his vice presidency, Bush was well-prepared to manage a smooth process for the ending of the Cold War during his administration. Simultaneously, Bush had to assess how US interests, opportunities, and challenges would shift going forward.

To guide US foreign policy after the Cold War, Bush proposed a grand strategy of a "New World Order." This international system would promote democracy worldwide through economic liberalization, multilateral diplomacy, and collective security, grounded in US power and leadership. When Iraq invaded Kuwait in the summer of 1990, the Bush administration applied the New World Order grand strategy—initially through diplomacy in Operation Desert Shield and then through military action in the Persian Gulf War, or Operation Desert Storm—to force Saddam Hussein's military forces out of Kuwait. The swift, six-week intervention and hundred-hour ground war appeared to demonstrate the success of Bush's new approach to US foreign policy and global security.

As the same time, as Dr. Bakich explains, Bush's grand strategy was ill-equipped to address the wide range of foreign-policy challenges after the Cold War, particularly problems of weak states that often led to humanitarian crises. Bush's New World Order was designed to address interstate conflict through collective security in a liberal international system, but it could not easily contend with intrastate disputes or nonstate actors. Consequently, Dr. Bakich concludes that the Persian Gulf War "was both a success and a failure. In narrow terms, the Gulf War was a military and diplomatic tour de force. . . . From a broader perspective, however, the war did not, and perhaps could not, facilitate Bush's grand ambitions." (Introduction, 7)

Dr. Bakich's compact and comprehensive analysis starts with a detailed study of Bush's professional background and its influence on his strategic worldview, which were widely shared by his national security team, before and during his presidency. The book then examines the Bush administration's initial overarching foreign policy review and development of the New World Order grand strategy. Next, the study examines the administration's application of the strategy to building an international coalition in response to Iraq's invasion of Kuwait, through diplomatic efforts and then military action. The book concludes with a thoughtful assessment of opportunities and limits for grand strategy after the Cold War.

This instructive study builds upon meticulous research in both scholarly and primary sources, including oral histories with administration officials and documents from the George H. W. Bush Presidential Library and other archives. Through examining the origins, goals, and application of Bush's New World Order, Dr. Bakich shows the cohesiveness that grand strategy aims to bring to policymaking as well as the difficulty of executing that cohesion with multiple state and nonstate actors. Understanding Bush's efforts to create a grand strategy for the post–Cold War era is essential to understanding the challenges of developing overarching policy doctrines in the twenty-first century.

Meena Bose
Hofstra University

ACKNOWLEDGMENTS

I could not have written this book without the support (material and moral) of many people. At the top of the list is Robert Strong. Not only did Bob read every sentence of this manuscript but he afforded me the opportunity to develop key components of the book's argument by inviting me to his institution, Washington and Lee University, to give a series of lectures on the Bush administration in 2019. Bob is in every way a gentleman scholar, and I am grateful for his sage counsel and steadfast support. Mike Nelson, too, pointed me in the right direction on numerous occasions, and with his incisive editorial pen, made my writing better. I should add that Mike's "On the ball!" email response to submitted work really does make my day. Brigadier Gen. Charles "Casey" Brower (USA, retired) read an early draft of the manuscript and made the invaluable suggestion that I consult Anatoly Chernyaev's memoir.

The Miller Center at the University of Virginia is a peerless institution for the study of the American presidency. I am indebted to Bill Antholis, Russell Riley, Marc Selverstone, and especially Barbara Perry for allowing me to contribute to the Miller Center's work. The Presidential Oral History Project is a national academic treasure; this book benefited tremendously from the George H. W. Bush project's transcripts. I am rewarded on a weekly basis by my conversations with my Miller Center fellow fellows, including John Owen, Dale Copeland, Ambassador Eric Edelman, Phil Potter, Todd Sechser, Allan Stam, Ambassador William Taylor, Brantly Womack, Shirley Lin, and Harry Harding, among many others. Jeff Legro, Allen Lynch, Philip Zelikow, and Melvyn Leffler (all UVA faculty or faculty alumni) played significant, if indirect, roles in the development of this book—all were instrumental in my thinking about the Bush presidency.

My colleagues and students at the Virginia Military Institute (VMI) are exceptional. In many ways, this book is an outgrowth of two courses I have offered in the International Studies Department since 2016, Contemporary US Grand Strategy and Strategy and Power. I am fortunate to spend my days with Dennis Foster, Patrick Rhamey, Brent Hierman, Ryan Holston, Vera Heuer, Tim Passmore, Megan Roosevelt, and Salih

Yasun. Dennis, Patrick, and Brent each spurred me to think more creatively about grand strategy, presidential decision-making, and America's relations with the Soviet Union and Russia. VMI provided much appreciated support for conference travel and this book's index.

I owe debts of gratitude to many others who read and commented on my work in progress. Among them are Will Walldorf, Ron Gurantz, Joel Campbell, Christopher Darnton, and especially Steve Bragaw and Joel Hillison. David Congdon and his stellar team at the University Press of Kansas were wonderful partners in this endeavor. I appreciate their professionalism and diligence.

Two nonacademic institutions provided me with dedicated time and space to get much of the manuscript completed. Thank you to Cavalier Aquatics and the Crozet Gators Swim Team for giving up a table and a bit of room on the deck to work.

Finally, my family is an undiminishing source of joy and inspiration. My brilliant wife, Kate, has the uncanny ability to know when I need to write and when I need to get out of the basement. I am grateful for her unflagging support and love. My boys, Jack and Aiden (order chosen by coin toss), are amazing people who never cease to surprise me with their insights and wisdom. They keep me focused on all that truly matters in life. My parents, Kris and Rus, and my brother, Trent, have given me so much. Seeing this manuscript bound will make them happy and proud, especially my dad. It is to him that this book is dedicated.

Introduction

In the summer of 1990 Iraqi president Saddam Hussein confronted a host of challenges to his rule and to his country's position in the Middle East. From 1980 to 1988, Iraq waged a brutal war with Iran that resulted in the deaths of some 150,000 to 180,000 Iraqi soldiers and put Saddam's government in debt to its Arab neighbors to the tune of $80 billion.[1] At a cost of roughly $450 billion, the toll of the Iran-Iraq War severely strained Iraq's economy at a time when dictatorships around the world were being toppled by popular uprisings. The Soviet Union, Iraq's long-time patron, was proving less supportive as its leader Mikhail Gorbachev focused on bettering relations with the United States. American influence in the Middle East was on the rise, too, resulting in warmer relations between the United States, Egypt, and Saudi Arabia. For a leader whose position required firm control of the levers of power, this confluence of events appeared threatening. But Saddam had a plan.

To orchestrate a reversal of fortune, Saddam would invade Kuwait, a country whose government was "generally unloved" in the Middle East and whose legitimacy—at least in Saddam's eyes—was tenuous at best.[2] Saddam believed that through conquest he could grab the mantle of pan-Arab leadership and secure for Iraq a commanding position in a new Middle East, erasing the debts he owed to the Kuwaiti government along the way. "In Saddam's world view," the editors of the *Saddam Tapes* write, "the pan-Arab dream could be achieved only when the center pole in the tent was firmly planted in Baghdad and protected by a heroic leader in the mold of Saladin, Nebuchadnezzar, or Hammurabi."[3]

Critically, Saddam reasoned, the time was ripe for his grand move: he believed that the world's attention was riveted to the changes ongoing in Europe and in the relationship between the United States and the Soviet Union; that the Soviets still had the wherewithal to back his play; and that Saudi Arabia and Egypt would rush to the pan-Arab banner that he would soon hoist. Unfortunately for the Iraqi leader, all these assessments proved incorrect.[4]

Officials in Washington watched with growing concern as Iraq's military forces began preparations for a possible attack. By late July 1990, policymakers in the George H. W. Bush administration understood that Saddam could launch an invasion without warning. Yet, no strong cautionary signals were sent from Washington to Baghdad. Saddam was bluffing, America's Arab partners insisted, and hostile rhetoric from the United States could provoke him into taking the step that everyone wished he would avoid.[5] When the invasion did occur on August 6, however, policymakers in the White House and State Department were quick to respond.

The first order of business was the implementation of a coercive diplomacy campaign designed, first, to deter Iraqi aggression against another state (most likely Saudi Arabia), and second, to compel Saddam to withdraw his forces from Kuwait by means short of war. Toward that end, President Bush and Secretary of State James Baker constructed a sizable international coalition of states that, in various combinations, provided political support for a host of UN Security Council resolutions aimed at coercing Iraq, contributed financial resources to the effort, and offered military forces for use in a war that seemed increasingly likely as time went on.[6] Operation Desert Shield, the name of the prewar military deployment of coalition forces to Saudi Arabia, was a massive undertaking that by October resulted in Saddam confronting roughly half a million coalition troops poised to evict the Iraqi military from Kuwait.[7] To make matters worse for Saddam, all the Arab states in the region, except Jordan, joined the coalition. Still, Saddam was unmoved.

Operation Desert Storm began on January 17 with a thirty-nine-day air campaign that quickly achieved command of the skies and, through punishing aerial bombardment, destroyed much of Iraq's combat power in the Kuwaiti Theater of Operations (KTO). By one estimate, roughly

40 percent of Iraqi armored vehicles were neutralized by coalition aircraft.[8] The ground campaign began on February 24 with two US Marine divisions crossing into Kuwait from Saudi Arabia with the intention of fixing Iraqi forces in place. Meanwhile, the coalition's main effort entailed a massive envelopment of Saddam's forces in Iraq, a maneuver known as "the left hook." The combined effect was devastating to Iraq's military, resulting in one of the most lopsided victories in military history. In the process, US forces demonstrated their superiority across the levels of war: tactical, operational, and theater-level strategy. On display was the American military's mastery of a style of warfare known as the "modern system," a combination of cover, concealment, fire, movement, and combined arms warfare, which when integrated with advanced target acquisition and standoff strike technologies obliterated much of Iraq's Republican Guard.[9] Owing to both the quality of American combat vehicles and the use of space-based intelligence and navigational systems (e.g., GPS), coalition forces could maneuver precisely at distances and speeds unmatched by Iraqi forces.[10] Taking advantage of the long border Iraq shares with Saudi Arabia, senior military officers extended the battlefield deep into Iraqi territory to implement a campaign designed to encircle and attrit a sizable percentage of the opponent's combat power.[11] Further, it should be noted that in addition to enforcing a stringent blockade, coalition naval forces contributed to the ground campaign by providing fires from platforms at sea. In the end, coalition forces pushed the Iraqi army out of Kuwait, destroyed thousands of tanks and armored personnel carriers, and killed or wounded tens of thousands of Iraqi soldiers.[12] By contrast, the United States lost 148 soldiers in battle. Its performance in the Persian Gulf War clearly illustrated the extent of the United States' conventional military primacy at the dawn of the post–Cold War era.

Among the wars fought by the United States since World War II, the Persian Gulf War is an oddity. Unlike the wars waged in Korea, Vietnam, Afghanistan, and Iraq (2003–2011), the Gulf War can be chalked up as a win, militarily and diplomatically, for the United States.[13] This war was far shorter, too, lasting weeks rather than years, and (not coincidentally) garnering a substantial amount of domestic political support.[14] From this perspective, the war to liberate Kuwait from Iraqi occupation resembles America's short and successful interventions in the Balkans a few years later. The differences there, however, are significant. Whereas the Bosnia and Kosovo wars involved principally American air power, the Gulf War entailed a massive mobilization and deployment of all forms of conventional forces. The Gulf War was also a global affair in ways that the more regionally contained conflicts in the Balkans were not. In short, for the United States the Gulf War was big, quick, and seemingly successful; it was, in a word, different.

Still, unlike in sports where wins, losses, and ties are easy to identify, the outcome of a war isn't always clear-cut. It was in World War II. Imperial Japan lost soundly. By August 1945 the Japanese military could no longer defend against an invasion of its remaining territory by the United States and the Soviet Union, and its civilian population could be subject to further incendiary and nuclear bombardment. Faced with this reality, Japan conceded defeat and submitted to occupation and the complete overhaul of its regime. The outcome of World War II in the Pacific (and in Europe) was a grand strategic victory for the United States and its allies, a victory so thorough that no one questioned the outcome years later.[15]

By contrast, the outcome of the Persian Gulf War was the subject of extensive second guessing almost as soon as the shooting stopped. Throughout the 1990s many scholars and policymakers argued that although Iraq was defeated on the battlefield, Saddam remained a threat to American interests in the region. The war seemed to have no effect on Saddam's willingness to behave provocatively. In 1991 the Iraqi military brutally suppressed Shi'a and Kurdish uprisings in Iraq's south and north, respectively; in 1994 Iraqi forces again mobilized in the south in what looked to be preparations for a repeat invasion of Kuwait; and in 1998, after what was interpreted as a pattern of obstructionism, Saddam declared an end to his country's cooperation with UN and International Atomic Energy Agency weapons inspectors. All the while, Saddam's rhetoric remained belligerent, as he claimed repeatedly that it was the Iraqis who prevailed in the Gulf War and not the Americans. From this point of view, the United States may have won the war, but it lost the peace.

Political scientist Joshua Rovner finds this argument unpersuasive.

First, Rovner notes that all four American objectives in the war were achieved: ejecting Iraq's military from Kuwait, restoring Kuwaiti sovereignty, protecting US citizens abroad, and promoting security and stability in the Gulf region. The United States and its allies successfully coerced Saddam into making concessions that he refused before the war and, through a brute force military campaign, dismantled the Iraqi military and economy to the point where Iraq's neighbors were no longer threatened. Most importantly, Saddam's behavior, while brutal toward his fellow Iraqis and petulant toward the United States, fundamentally changed in ways that served US national interests in the region for years to come. Prior to the war, Saddam was externally focused, seeking to aggrandize his power under a pan-Arab scheme; after the conflict, he was preoccupied by internal threats to his power and therefore posed few if any challenges to the stability of the region. While it is true that the international community maintained the biting economic sanctions on Iraq and that American and British military action was used to "keep Saddam in his box," the reality of the US victory in the Persian Gulf War is unassailable.[16]

This line of analysis is important for two related reasons. First, by providing a framework for evaluating strategic success and failure, Rovner identifies and corrects flaws in the conventional wisdom that had developed over time. Importantly, Rovner doesn't simply mark the war's end point and declare a winner at that moment; rather, he extends his view years after the war to evaluate its longer-term effects. Such a perspective allows him to assess whether (and for how long) the outcome of the Persian Gulf War satisfied American national security interests. Second, Rovner's analysis shows how misperceptions about victory and defeat can lead to flawed assessments about an opponent's intentions and capabilities in the future. By 1998, many American policymakers had come to believe the hype about Saddam being the real winner of the Gulf War, and this belief in turn made them more sympathetic to the idea that American security could be enhanced only through a war for regime change.[17]

And yet, Rovner's analysis misses an important factor that made war in the Gulf necessary to George H. W. Bush, affected his choices for how the war would be fought, and influenced his decision to end the war:

American grand strategy, or the higher order framework that guided the Bush administration's statecraft and ultimately determined the political purposes the war was supposed to serve. A thoroughgoing analysis of the Persian Gulf War must begin and end with an accurate contextualization of the conflict in terms of what the Bush administration was attempting to achieve in the world—not just in the region—and how it worked to secure those big objectives. The war to liberate Kuwait in 1991 occurred at a moment of epochal significance in world history, as the bipolar Cold War standoff between the United States and Soviet Union was coming to an end. How American officials sought to manage the Cold War's endgame, and crucially, what type of system—or global order—they attempted to build to replace the old one, conditioned their views on where, when, how, and why military force should be used. Rather than asking "Did America win the Persian Gulf War?" this book poses another set of questions. First, what grand strategic objectives did Bush seek in America's effort to reverse Iraq's invasion of its smaller neighbor? Second, how did Bush's grand strategy influence the ways in which the United States confronted Iraq? Third, what were the effects of the Gulf War on American grand strategy during the transition from one era to another?

This book's main argument is that the Persian Gulf War was a product of what I term George Bush Senior's "New World Order grand strategy." Developed in spring 1989, the New World Order grand strategy aimed to foster democracy in Central and Eastern Europe, move beyond containment by incentivizing the Soviet Union's continued liberalization and inclusion in the Western democratic capitalist system, and establish a new global order wherein multilateral diplomacy and collective security would be facilitated by American power and leadership. Saddam Hussein's invasion of Kuwait threatened Bush's vision of global order in the emerging post–Cold War era. At the same time, Bush recognized the Persian Gulf crisis as an opportunity to further strengthen Soviet-American relations and reinvigorate collective security under United Nations auspices. Bush's coercive diplomacy campaign, Operation Desert Shield, and ultimate decision for war, Operation Desert Storm, were directly connected to his grand strategy for managing the end of the Cold War and transitioning to a new model of interstate relations.

Just as Bush's grand strategy affected the decision for, and conduct of, the Gulf War, its aftermath had grand strategic consequences. Due to the ad hoc nature of the war's termination, which left Saddam with sufficient military resources to commit atrocities on Iraq's Kurdish and Shi'a populations, the United States and its allies were compelled to sustain military operations against Iraq long after it was expelled from Kuwait. The continued use of American power had a pernicious effect on others' perceptions of US intentions in the region. The challenges that the United States confronted, moreover, were not of a type envisioned by Bush's grand strategy. Humanitarian disasters brought on by weak and failing states, rather than interstate aggression, proved to be the norm in the early years of the post–Cold War era. In many respects, the Gulf War's aftermath demonstrated that Bush's grand strategic initiative was ill-suited to the challenges in the emerging system. In grand strategic terms, then, the Persian Gulf War was paradoxical. Intended to be the catalyst for a revived liberal international order that rested on a foundation of collective security among the great powers, the conflict helped to undermine the prospects of that very order.

What we must reckon with—but not, in the end, reconcile—is that the war was both a success and a failure. In narrow terms, the Gulf War was a military and diplomatic tour de force. The sources of America's military-diplomatic success lie in the way in which President Bush and his senior officials fashioned a coherent and comprehensive strategy for the war, one that leveraged American power and influence to achieve aims that were properly circumscribed and which effectively marshalled domestic support. From a broader perspective, however, the war did not, and perhaps could not, facilitate Bush's grand ambitions. This duality makes the Persian Gulf War both fascinating and worthy of study.

The Road Ahead

Over the course of the next five chapters, I will make the case that George Bush's New World Order grand strategy guided the decision for war against Saddam Hussein's Iraq and determined the military and diplomatic strategies for waging that war. Chapter 1 discusses Bush's attributes as a strategist. Attention is paid, first, to Bush's strategic beliefs about America's role in an international system undergoing profound change. These beliefs are critical for understanding how the Bush administration formulated strategy, specifically how it assessed the international security environment, understood the utility of available resources, and assessed costs and risks of potential foreign policy initiatives. Bush's strategic beliefs are also important because his administration's system of decision-making placed him firmly at the center of US statecraft, empowering—rather than diluting—his influence in the crafting of American grand strategy.

Chapter 2 addresses American grand strategy from January 1989 to August 1990, the period from Bush's inauguration to Iraq's invasion of Kuwait. The president's vision was predicated on liberal democratic norms, collective security, and American leadership. While Bush fashioned this approach as he managed relations with the Soviet Union and Europe, the chapter also addresses US relations with other regions, including Asia, Latin America, and the Middle East. To a considerable extent, the overriding goal of the Bush administration's policies toward the non-European world was the mitigation of risk posed to its efforts aimed at managing the end of the Cold War on US terms.

Chapter 3 demonstrates how Bush's New World Order grand strategy directly affected his decision to confront Iraq after its invasion of Kuwait. As much as it weakened regional security and threatened American interests in the Middle East, Saddam's invasion of Kuwait undermined core elements of the US initiative for world order. Seen in this context, Bush's determination to confront Iraq by working through the United Nations and to create a broad international coalition in support of American objectives, as well as his repeated overtures to Soviet leaders to participate militarily in the coalition, were fundamental (rather than peripheral) to his strategic response to crisis in the Gulf. Additionally, this chapter explains how American military deployments were tightly aligned with the administration's diplomatic efforts to exert significant pressure on Saddam.

Chapter 4 covers the course of Operation Desert Storm and the reasons why Bush decided to terminate the war early. I first examine the development of the US military's campaign plan, illustrating how intimately involved Bush and his senior advisers were in this process and how Bush's grand strategic objectives influenced the military's decision-making. Additionally, this chapter shows how the timing of the ground attack phase was influenced by diplomatic developments, specifically Gorbachev's ultimately futile efforts to mediate the conflict before the land war commenced. Finally, Bush's decision to terminate the war early is considered. The product of intense time pressures and cross-cutting imperatives, the decision ultimately prevented the United States from locking in many of the grand strategic objectives embodied in its war aims.

Finally, chapter 5 evaluates the longer-term effects of the war on Bush's New World Order grand strategy. Saddam's political survival and brutal suppression of internal challengers to his regime necessitated the continued use of force by the United States and Britain in the form of two no-fly zones over Iraq. The potential for Saddam to threaten American partners in the region, moreover, meant that America's military presence would remain long after the war. This permanent display of America power ran counter to Bush's grand strategic vision. Separately, Gorbachev's political fortunes declined after the war, and the Soviet Union collapsed in December 1991. The combination of the Gulf War's messy ending and the loss of a trusted partner in Moscow undermined Bush's strategy to create a particular world order for the post–Cold War era.

CHAPTER 1

George Bush: President and Strategist

By the time he ran for the presidency in 1988, George H. W. Bush was widely viewed as Ronald Reagan's natural successor. His two terms as Reagan's vice president were but the most recent entries on Bush's lengthy list of professional accomplishments. He had spent the 1970s serving as the US ambassador to the United Nations, the chief of the US Liaison Office (USLO) to China, and the director of Central Intelligence (DCI). These experiences shaped his strategic beliefs. A deeply committed internationalist by the time he assumed the vice presidency, Bush came to this perspective for pragmatic reasons in 1964. That year, after losing his first bid for a seat in the US Senate from Texas, Bush concluded that the dogmatic "right wingers" and isolationist elements in the Republican Party contributed not only to his electoral defeat but also to the drubbing the GOP suffered nationally that year.[1] Over the course of the next fifteen years, Bush's fidelity to internationalism would strengthen and grow in sophistication as his exposure to foreign affairs and national security policy widened.

Richard Nixon's decision to tap him to serve as the US ambassador to the UN in the spring of 1971 wasn't what Bush hoped for (he would have preferred to be nominated to head the Treasury Department); nor was Bush seen as an appropriate choice for that position by many commentators. "There seems to be nothing in his record that qualifies him for this highly important position," the *New York Times* editorialized. Harsher still was the opinion of the *Washington Star*, which declared Nixon's decision "the appointment of a political loser."[2] Taken at face value, these charges had some merit. Bush knew little about foreign affairs and he had just lost his candidacy for a seat in the Senate. Yet, Bush possessed two attributes that would allow him to gain competency in the world of diplomacy: a politician's skills in retail politics and a willingness to adapt to the rules and norms of the institutions of which he was now a part.

Bush was never eloquent or comfortable when addressing large audiences. He did, however, excel in cultivating personal relationships, and at the UN he developed his own style of diplomacy. Bush hosted and toasted his fellow representatives and dignitaries from around the world, treating them with respect, listening to their concerns, and carefully considering their perspectives. As his contacts expanded and personal relationships with his fellow diplomats grew, Bush came to appreciate that above all else his fellow representatives deeply valued their nations' sovereignty rights. Others knew this, of course, but Bush saw the attachment to the norm of sovereignty as key to finding common ground with his colleagues from other countries. He believed that by showing his counterparts that he—and by extension, the US government—respected them personally, he could create opportunities for cooperation and smooth over diplomatic frictions when times got tough. Bush quickly discovered that he needed to engage with representatives from all states (irrespective of the size or significance to US policy) because smaller countries had begun voting in blocs, a development that magnified their influence in the UN. The onus was thus on the American ambassador to build relationships early to navigate the institution more effectively.[3] By the time he left his post, Bush's commitment to the UN was deep, as were his appreciation for the value others placed in their own state's sovereignty and his determination to work collaboratively with actors of all (or most) stripes.

Bush left the United Nations in January 1973 to take on one of the most difficult jobs imaginable at the time, the chairmanship of the Republican National Committee during the era of the Watergate scandal. Never an insider in Nixon's White House, Bush had no role in the constitutional crisis that would ultimately cost Nixon the presidency, but it was his job as the RNC chair to defend the president in the court of public opinion. By all accounts, he did so honestly to the extent that

Nixon repeatedly professed his innocence to Bush. Yet by virtue of his position, Bush was responsible for promoting the Republican brand at a time when the country was losing faith in the institutions of government. He thus faced incessant and draining hostility from the public and press. Over the course of twenty-one months as chair of the RNC, Bush learned how damaging the loss of domestic support could be for a president and his agenda.[4]

Scarred by the experience of defending the indefensible, Bush longed for a change in role and location. In 1974 the newly inaugurated president Gerald Ford offered Bush one of two of the choicest diplomatic posts available, an ambassadorship either to London or Paris. Bush turned them both down, choosing instead to be America's chief representative to the People's Republic of China. This choice would have a tremendous impact on Bush's life and on the development of his strategic beliefs. Because the United States and China did not have formal relations, Washington was without ambassadorial-level representation in Beijing. As such, Bush headed the USLO (though he retained the title of ambassador due to his prior service at the UN). From Beijing, Bush viewed the international scene from a radically different vantage point than his State Department colleagues in Washington. The world Bush witnessed was undergoing significant transformation: Soviet-American relations were under increasing strain and détente was being attacked from both the left and right in the United States; the Sino-Soviet split was complete, but the honeymoon between the United States and China had ended; and the denouement of the long-running conflict in Vietnam was unfolding in dramatic fashion. Bush's time in China offered him distance from the fallout of Watergate and the opportunity to acquire a richness and depth of knowledge about the world and America's place in it.

Bush had every intention of using his own brand of personal diplomacy in China to further improve Sino-American relations following the opening forged by Nixon and Kissinger. Yet, events conspired against him. First, Bush was posted to China during the Cultural Revolution, a time when the PRC was convulsed by radicalism and violence. His freedom of maneuver in the capital city was restricted, and the Chinese government had little intention of making any interlocutors available for him to engage on a personal level.[5] Leaders in Beijing were suffering from a case of "Middle Kingdom Syndrome," which precluded relationship building at a time when Bush believed they were most needed.⁶ Anti-American rhetoric, moreover, was a constant in Chinese propaganda. Although Bush understood that to a certain extent the vitriol was intended to shore up the domestic legitimacy of the Chinese Communist Party, he feared that Beijing's constant criticisms would undermine US domestic political support for any partnership with the PRC. Bush believed that both countries would benefit from a steady drumbeat of positive stories touting improvements in their relationship. By casting US-Chinese relations in a positive light, Bush hoped to create a feeling of progress among the American people, a foundation on which genuine progress could be made. Barred from spending significant time with Chinese officials, however, Bush could only practice personal diplomacy with other states' representatives in Beijing.⁷

State Department officials in Washington further limited Bush's ability to engage in extensive personal diplomacy with officials in Beijing. As the USLO chief, Bush was beholden to the policies of Secretary of State Kissinger, who dominated foreign policymaking during the year Bush was in China. The consummate practitioner of realpolitik, Kissinger rejected the idea that personal trust among government officials mattered in diplomacy. Far more relevant to the secretary of state were the balance of interests and the degree to which power could be leveraged to create effective bargaining positions. Bush's plan to generate a steady stream of positive stories about Sino-American relations directly contradicted Kissinger's desire to stall progress in the relationship, an effort designed to enhance Washington's leverage over Beijing. Bush could do little except toe the line Kissinger set for him and his staff.⁸

In fact, there were scant opportunities for an official of Bush's stature to affect Kissinger's agenda given the secretary of state's near complete centralization of the foreign policy decision-making process. Bush bore the brunt of this operating style, concluding that Kissinger's modus operandi posed significant risks to the country's interests. As Bush confided to his diary in November 1974, "I am wondering if it is good for our country to have as much individual diplomacy. Isn't the President best served if the important matters are handled by more than one person?"⁹ The problem, as Bush witnessed firsthand, was that Kissinger's tight control over foreign policy turned otherwise able staffers into cowed functionaries who spent their time attending to the secretary's whims.

Observing Kissinger and his entourage in Beijing, Bush noted, "His staff is scared to death of him. The procession is almost 'regal.' People quake: 'He's coming. He's coming.' And don't dare tell him when he's keeping them waiting."[10] Reflecting on the restrictions Kissinger placed on the USLO in China, Bush lamented, "It is difficult to define what our function is here."[11]

Moreover, while Bush disagreed with some of Kissinger's policies, he considered the secretary of state's style downright dangerous. As Brent Scowcroft, national security adviser to President Ford and then eventually to Bush himself, summarized, "What he [Bush] learned from Kissinger was 'don't depend on only one single voice, no matter how good that one voice is.' That's not the way he thought he ought to get his information [while president] . . . what he wanted was to hear strong people, knowledgeable people, argue points of view in front of him."[12]

It was from China that Bush viewed the fall of Saigon in April 1975. In his view, the violent and chaotic collapse of the South Vietnamese regime could not be separated from the anti-American rhetoric emanating from Beijing's propaganda outlets. An adherent to the so-called domino theory, Bush believed that American credibility in the eyes of allies and adversaries was critical to securing US national priorities, based on the premise that as more of its allies and partners around the world questioned America's capacity and determination to lead, the more likely its adversaries would be to step into the breach and exert influence at odds with US interests. Reflecting on the state of Southeast Asia policy, Bush noted that "as the United States has reneged on commitments and pulled back . . . the free countries [in Southeast Asia] are concerned . . . These countries cannot depend on the U.S. any longer and thus they have to look toward Russia or more likely China."[13] Bush feared the erosion of freedom globally and believed that only the United States could serve as the bulwark against communist expansion. Yet he did not advocate ideological crusades; he understood that effective leadership depended on a credible and rational strategy that entailed sound, defensible commitments. The fall of Saigon was a blow to US credibility and leadership. Shoring up America's global position would require an honest assessment of which of its commitments were worth defending and which needed to be jettisoned.

Whereas Kissinger's approach to decision-making highlighted the risk of excessive centralization, Bush's service as DCI demonstrated the perils of intelligence politicization. Ford recalled Bush from China in December 1975, tapping him for DCI at a time when the CIA was under intense congressional scrutiny for a litany of misdeeds committed throughout the 1960s and 1970s. The CIA was also being attacked by hawks on the right who alleged that the agency was dangerously misguided in its assessments of Soviet capabilities and intentions. From their perch on the President's Foreign Intelligence Advisory Board (PFIAB), a group of CIA critics pressed Ford, Kissinger, and Bush to allow for a "competitive" estimate of Soviet behavior, one that would ostensibly balance out the picture of the Soviet threat.[14] Bush's deputy director George Carver warned him that the PFIAB members were not committed to the best available truth about Soviet intentions. Rather, they were acting according to their shared conviction that "intelligence officers should deliberately try to shape policy by calling attention to the worst things the Soviets could do in order to stimulate appropriate countermeasure responses by the U.S. Government."[15] The resulting "Team B" estimate was unsurprising in its substance, flawed in its methodology, wrong in its conclusions, and corrosive to the professional estimative process.[16] Bush had been alerted to the dangers of politicization, but he also wanted to minimize factionalism in the Republican foreign policy establishment, a trend that was well under way as the anti-détente critics on the political right gained voice.[17] The whole affair did, however, reinforce in Bush's mind the value of the expertise of the CIA (and other government agencies).[18] It also showed him that absent an honest and professional process, intelligence and decision-making could be corrupted. As he confessed to Ford, Kissinger, and Secretary of Defense Donald Rumsfeld at the Ford administration's last NSC meeting, "I feel like I've been had."[19]

George Bush was not a movement conservative. His battle against Ronald Reagan in the 1980 Republican primary caused many on the right to question whether he was, in fact, a conservative at all. Reagan, too, confessed at being "pissed off" when on the campaign trail Bush described Reagan's so-called supply side economic policies as "voodoo economics." Reagan nevertheless agreed to have Bush on the Republican ticket, and the political partnership the two formed proved highly effective. Bush both prized and exhibited loyalty. As vice president, he never sought opportunities to outshine Reagan or to create the impression that there was any daylight between the two of them. Bush proved to be an absolute administration loyalist whom Reagan came to trust.[20] The vice president was invited into Reagan's inner circle of adviser and remained at the president's side throughout Reagan's two terms in office, offering the president his counsel in private.[21]

National security decision-making in the Reagan White House was often shambolic, riven by personal feuds among the chief policymakers and beset with structural dysfunction. Early in Reagan's first term, the decision was made to downgrade the role of the national security adviser. As presidential counselor Edwin Meese described, the national security adviser "will be a staff person and act like a staff person. He will be much less visible. He will be a coordinator and the NSC staff will be used as a coordinating vehicle rather than to formulate foreign policy."[22] The national security adviser's reduced status was part of the administration's goal of establishing a "cabinet government" wherein the special assistant to the president would not be seen as equal in stature to either the secretary of state or secretary of defense.[23] Under this configuration, Richard Allen, Reagan's first national security adviser, had to have the approval of Chief of Staff James Baker, Baker's deputy Michael Deaver, and Meese to see the president for any reason other than his scheduled morning intelligence briefing. Meanwhile, relations among the president's foreign policy team were exceedingly poor. The high-strung and turf obsessed Secretary of State Al Haig proved difficult to work with and eventually lost influence in the administration. George Shultz, Haig's replacement, and Secretary of Defense Caspar Weinberger disagreed on most issues.[24] Absent a trusted and influential national security adviser who could manage their disputes, decisions were delayed and policies went uncoordinated.

Reagan's policy process amounted to a constellation of four coordinating committees for defense, intelligence, foreign policy, and crisis management. Over Haig's objections, George Bush was selected to chair the crisis management committee. In the summer of 1981, that committee became the National Security Planning group, "a kind of NSC-plus" that dealt with a range of crises, including the *Achille Lauro* incident of October 1985.[25]

Reagan recognized, too, that Bush was an effective representative of his administration's policies abroad. The president frequently sent Bush to meet with America's European allies, and to the Soviet Union and China, to discuss matters that were critical to Reagan's policy agenda. In January 1983, for example, Bush visited seven European capitals to bolster allied support for the so-called zero-zero option, a proposed arms control framework that would have the Soviets withdraw all their intermediate-range SS-20 missiles in Eastern Europe in exchange for a cancellation of the proposed American deployment of Pershing IIs. The Soviets rejected this initiative on the grounds that it was imbalanced (i.e., the Soviets would withdraw missiles already deployed, whereas the Americans would have to withdraw only the proposal to deploy the Pershing IIs). Bush's mission was to explain to America's allies—whose leaders were facing domestic political resistance to a possible deployment of a new class of nuclear missiles—that Reagan's policy was designed to induce the Soviets to accept a solution that would ultimately result in fewer weapons deployed to Europe. The trip was a success. The vice president managed to put "a reasonable face on American policy," defusing "Reagan's image as a nuclear cowboy."[26]

Reagan used Bush's diplomatic talents to build the administration's relations with China; he also tasked him to represent the United States at the funerals of Leonid Brezhnev, Yuri Andropov, and Konstantin Chernenko—three general secretaries of the Soviet Union who passed away in rapid succession.[27] At these (and other) funerals, Bush employed his style of diplomacy aimed at building rapport and trust with leaders from around the world. "Truthfully," Bush explained in his diary, "these funerals often resulted in many useful bilateral meetings with the incoming leaders."[28] Along with Shultz, Bush was the first American official to meet the newly appointed general secretary Mikhail Gorbachev. At the conclusion of their meeting in March 1985, Bush was uncertain whether Gorbachev would simply be a more effective (and youthful) spokesperson for stale Soviet foreign policies, or if Gorbachev genuinely sought to "start new" in US-Soviet relations. Bush urged Reagan to test the sincerity of Gorbachev's intent to forge a new relationship. It was worth a shot, Bush noted, "as the monkey said when he was shot into space, 'it beats the hell out of the cancer lab'."[29]

George Bush's seventeen-year foreign policy education was remarkable in the history of the American presidency. That curriculum—which included service as ambassador to the United Nations and China, director of Central Intelligence, and vice president of the United States—prepared him exceptionally well for the presidency. It was these experiences, moreover, that formed the set of strategic beliefs that would guide his actions at a pivotal moment in world history.

Bush's Strategic Beliefs

Bush had formed a nuanced view of international politics by the time he was elected president. Though a champion of US global leadership, Bush was cognizant of the limits of America's power and influence. He believed, moreover, that radical change was as dangerous as it was alluring; yet he considered the use of force (the vehicle most likely to bring about dramatic transformation) as being necessary under a range of conditions. A leader often described as prudent and pragmatic, Bush also concluded that American security and world peace could both be significantly enhanced by a thorough refashioning of the global order. These seemingly contrasting aspects of Bush's worldview are not inherently contradictory. They are a reflection, rather, of his understanding of a complex international system.

Bush possessed a keen sense of strategic empathy, the ability to place himself in another leader's shoes and view the world from her or his perspective. This empathy allowed him to envision both the opportunities for action and the ways in which good fortune could turn bad. Due in part to his appreciation of the intricacies of interstate relations, Bush preferred steadiness over abrupt change, saw threats lurking in uncertainty and instability, and believed that American leadership was essential to securing his country and its allies—and to promoting world peace. Yet, Bush's strategic beliefs were traditional insofar as they reflected the embedded norms and conventions of the world he inhabited. That world was made up of states whose leaders he could engage through personal diplomacy, whether to manage crises or to capitalize on burgeoning opportunities.

Given America's outsized role in global affairs and the inherent limits of its power, US policy had to be guided by an overarching strategic discipline that carefully aligned means and ends. The lesson Bush took from the fall of Saigon was that the United States had to have a sense of proportion in its foreign policy if it were to recover its global influence. America had to defend its commitments, but those commitments had to be chosen wisely. How the United States made good on its commitments mattered as well. Bush held a multifaceted conception of power, an understanding that US interests were best secured through a synergistic employment of the nation's resources.[30] As a strategist, Bush sought solvency in American statecraft. He understood that resources could be drained in the pursuit of goals that were either too grand or too numerous. Bush also sensed that American foreign policy would succeed only if its diplomatic, military, and economic policies complemented each other. Diplomacy was needed to contextualize military might; military power served as the backstop to effective American diplomacy; both were significantly affected by the health of the US economy.

Bush was not a foreign policy realist. To the contrary, he believed that American interests were best secured by working through multilateral institutions, fostering free trade, and promoting democracy abroad.[31] Yet, those liberal mechanisms neither emerged naturally nor functioned automatically. American leadership was essential.[32] To Bush, the United States' relationship with its allies and partners was one of primus inter pares. Furthermore, Bush's internationalism envisioned the creation and maintenance of stable international conditions that permitted states (adversaries and allies alike) to work cooperatively and allowed democracy and free trade to flourish over time.[33] When he considered opportunities for expanding American influence and commitments—in either the economic or political dimensions—Bush's preferred approach was incremental and institutional. Beneficial trading relations were to be gained not by aggressive "open door" policies but through multilateral arrangements.[34] Democracy, moreover, was best secured by those who sought and struggled for it. The United States played an important role by setting an example for others to follow and by creating conditions that steered clear of adverse, possibly violent, reactions by antidemocratic forces.[35] Bush believed, in other words, that radically transformative policies were likely to be counterproductive. Far better to work for stability in international politics, to seek a measure of predictability in the relations among states that allowed liberalizing trends to grow over time.

Bush's strategic discipline informed his foreign policy liberalism. He believed, for example, that working with allies and through international institutions enabled the United States to sustain its power and influence abroad at reduced cost. Bush believed that if the United States recognized the legitimate security of interests of other states and pursued commonly held objectives, American security interests could be enhanced without breaking the bank. The United Nations was a powerful instrument of peace, and working through the UN would ultimately bolster America's core objectives. But the UN could only function effectively with strong American leadership, which should accommodate the perspectives and values of others states when possible so that more countries would support US initiatives. If outright support wasn't in the cards, then early engagement would, hopefully, lessen the obstructionism by those who could not agree with US policies.[36]

Bush's world view had a tragic sensibility, a recognition that things could go terribly wrong if American policymakers succumbed to dogma. Pragmatism, or in Bush's parlance "prudence," was the antidote. Bush's pragmatism accepted uncertainty in global affairs and fallibility in the people responsible for statecraft. Pragmatism demanded a commitment to results (however imperfect they may be), a continuous testing of assumptions, and a willingness to seek a diversity of views. Using US resources wisely and effectively depended on a president's willingness to entertain multiple perspectives and to wield various tools in the service of national goals. America, Bush believed, could achieve great things in the world; his objectives were, as we will see, bold.[37] But the path toward greatness was fraught and had to be tread carefully and wisely. As it navigated a dynamic and potentially dangerous world, America had to avoid acting in ways that did more harm than good.[38]

Bush's Foreign Policy Decision-Making Process

President Bush's strategic beliefs—his understanding of international political dynamics, the utility of America's power resources, and the value of information diversity—were shared by most of the senior officials in his administration. Bush's core group of advisers were all friends who worked exceptionally well together. The personal relationships among Bush, Secretary of State James Baker, Secretary of Defense Richard Cheney, and Scowcroft explain—in part—why the Bush administration functioned so harmoniously and effectively in foreign policy. More important, however, is how these individuals and the departments they led fit into a rigorous and competently run strategic decision-making process.

Bush tapped his best friend to run his presidential campaign and to serve as secretary of state. The Bush-Baker partnership, the product of a close, decades-long friendship, set the tone and direction of US foreign policy. Baker, like Bush, had an innate preference for stability and cooperation in international politics. If change was inevitable, Baker strove to make it evolutionary, not revolutionary. Baker was an immensely talented negotiator and dealmaker who sought to leverage his skills to America's benefit during revolutionary times. In managing relations with the Soviet Union, paving the way for German reunification, and confronting Saddam Hussein in the Persian Gulf, Baker's first instinct was to work with allies, partners, and anyone else he could cajole to support American policy. Baker understood, moreover, that his authority and influence flowed directly from the absolute faith and confidence that Bush had in him. Critical to Baker's diplomatic successes was the unquestionable bond between the president and secretary of state—a bond that Baker at times exploited to advance his agenda.[39] "I had a great advantage as Secretary of State, because I'd been a thirty-five-year friend with the president," Baker recalled. "I was his political adviser. Nobody was going to get in between me and my President.... I could go out and speak with authority 'cause everybody knew how close I was to President Bush 41."[40] Scowcroft, who was also very close to Bush, took steps to bolster Baker's authority by refusing to seek the limelight for himself and ensuring that the secretary of state would be the principal voice of American foreign policy.[41]

Notwithstanding Baker's position as America's top diplomat and the faith that the president had in his abilities, it was George Bush's strategic beliefs that determined the direction of US foreign policy. Baker was temperamentally a problem-solver, a trait admired by some, derided by others. "Kissinger saw himself as a geopolitical strategist and grand architect of history, a latter-day Metternich shaping the forces that guided the world," Peter Baker and Susan Glasser explained. "Baker, by contrast, gave little thought to the Treaty of Westphalia or the historical context of great-power competition. He was no professor. He was a problem solver, animated by the challenge of finding ways to get things done."[42]

Perhaps the best explanation of Baker's approach to foreign policy and his role in the administration's broader conduct of statecraft comes from Scowcroft:

> I was primarily concerned with the strategy of what we were doing. Baker was much more concerned with the tactics. When, for example, we would discuss issues of arms control and what we should propose to the president, Baker would almost always home in on the negotiability of what we wanted to do. And I didn't care much about that. I was interested in how we could change and improve the balance.[43]

This isn't to say that Baker was beholden to Scowcroft and the National Security Council Staff. In the diplomatic realm the Bush-Baker tandem was the "core steering mechanism" for foreign policy.[44] Together, Bush and Baker were instrumental in devising the administration's diplomatic initiatives. It fell to Scowcroft and his NSC staff to place these initiatives in a broader grand strategic context and, crucially, to make sure the administration's nondiplomatic policies aligned with the administration's diplomatic efforts (and vice versa). Baker's tactical orientation mattered significantly because it gave policy substance to Bush's strategic beliefs.

Bush's first choice to run the Department of Defense, the chairman of the Senate Armed Services Committee John Tower, was rejected by the Senate for a host of reasons pertaining to his personal conduct and cozy relationship with defense contractors.[45] Realizing the administration needed to fill the vacancy at the Pentagon quickly, Scowcroft and Bush turned to Dick Cheney, the House minority whip and fellow alumnus of the Ford administration. Substantively, Cheney's worldview was the furthest from Bush's among the president's closest advisers. Whereas Bush saw multilateral engagement as being essential to securing US national security interests, Cheney was far more of a unilateralist who had scant appreciation for the UN. And while Bush understood the need for cultivating congressional support for foreign policy, Cheney quickly grew to mistrust the legislative body he had just left, especially in the national security domain.[46] Further, where Bush had a balanced and sophisticated view of the instruments of national power, Cheney was much more enamored with US hard power assets, the American military above all else; he also believed that America should seek to maximize its relative power position over its principal rival, the Soviet Union.[47] Although Bush would be convinced eventually that Gorbachev's perestroika and "New Thinking" in Soviet foreign policy were genuine and that the general secretary was a valuable partner worthy of Washington's support, Cheney remained steadfast in his belief that America's approach to the Soviet Union had to be competitive and zero-sum.[48]

While these views made Cheney an ideological outlier in Bush's core group of advisers, he had long known Baker, Scowcroft, and Bush, and they worked well as a team. Policy differences among them were dealt with professionally, with little fanfare. The group's familiarity and trust enabled them to manage internal conflicts well below the boiling point.[49] Furthermore, these officials served a president who loathed the discord caused by petty bureaucratic fights. Bush laid down the law, demanding harmony and evincing a willingness to fire those who behaved in ways that threatened the cooperative ethos pervading the administration.

Soon after his confirmation, Cheney convinced Bush to tap Gen. Colin Powell to serve as chairman of the Joint Chiefs of Staff. Powell was not the obvious choice for the position. Not only was he junior to others in the armed forces, but he had recently finished serving a stint as Reagan's national security adviser. In most administrations, an officer with Powell's résumé would have had to wait at least until he had served a successful joint command posting before being tapped to be the president's senior military adviser. Nor did Cheney share Powell's view that the Cold War was, if not over, then certainly on its last legs. Yet, Cheney successfully advocated for Powell on the grounds that the two had a strong working relationship during the final two years of the Reagan administration. Powell would soon become the most influential chairman of the Joint Chiefs in US history, in part because of the Goldwater-Nichols reforms that imbued the position with significant authority and also because Cheney empowered Powell within the Pentagon and the White House.[50]

Bush wanted no team of rivals in the Lincoln mold advising him on policy. Yet, his choices of individuals to head the two most important national security departments created just that possibility. Baker and Cheney populated their departments with staffers who were intensely loyal to their respective bosses and who shared their worldviews. That the Bush administration did not devolve into bureaucratic infighting is testament not only to Baker's and Cheney's close personal ties but also to the role played by Bush's national security adviser, Brent Scowcroft.

National security advisers occupy the central position in the making of foreign and defense policy. Broadly speaking, these senior officials wear two hats. On the one hand, they are responsible for managing the foreign policy process, ensuring that the president is afforded a range of sound options, and coordinating the multitude of policy lines that cut across different agencies and departments. In this role, the national security adviser can be viewed with suspicion by the president's cabinet members because the efforts of the White House's NSC staff often conflict with departmental prerogatives and agendas. On the other hand, national security advisers have an advisory role, one that is unfettered by obligations to any department or agency. With ready access to the president, the national security adviser is often the first and last person to discuss foreign policy matters with the chief executive. These two roles can easily come into conflict, or be perceived to conflict, resulting in a breakdown in the strategic decision-making process and a decline in the quality of policy.[51]

Brent Scowcroft was no ordinary national security adviser. By virtue of their extraordinarily close professional relationship, Bush empowered Scowcroft to the hilt. Scowcroft's worldview was, moreover, very close to Bush's—so much so that NSC staffer Philip Zelikow remarked "there were times at which I thought Bush and Scowcroft were almost like two dimensions of the same person. He was almost like a kind of doppelganger for Bush."[52] Scowcroft offered Bush advice that was grand strategic in its perspective. Scowcroft "kept his eyes on the big picture," Bartholomew Sparrow explains, "observing events and developments around the world, anticipating how domestic and international factors interrelate, and calculating the best way for the United States to protect its national security and secure its own interests."[53] In line with Bush's strategic beliefs, Scowcroft believed multilateral engagement and working within international institutions were critical to securing US objectives. Working with others in institutional settings required strong US leadership, however. Unlike Cheney, but again like Bush, Scowcroft was skeptical of change that brought in its wake a significant amount of uncertainty. He held that America was most secure in a world that changed gradually. At the same time, both Bush and Scowcroft were comfortable with the use of military force if clear US security interests were at stake.

In important ways, though, Scowcroft was more of a realist than Bush. Bush's national security adviser "accepts the world as it is, a world in which tyranny, corruption, ethnic hatreds, and failed states persist. Consequently, he tolerates the moral failings of other regimes."[54] As a result, Scowcroft was less inclined to see the benefits of policies aimed at promoting democracy abroad. Bush, on the other hand, accepted the view that a world of democratic states was more conducive to US security.

As we have seen, Bush was determined to devise a foreign policy process free of the dysfunction he saw in the Nixon administration. Specifically, Bush desired a process that avoided excessive centralization, one that provided him with a diverse array of information from the national security bureaucracy. Bush was also intent to avoid the disorganization that characterized much of Reagan's first-term decision-making process. At the same time, he wanted to retain control of the foreign policy process, to ensure that his vision guided American statecraft. The task of threading this needle fell to Scowcroft, arguably the best suited person at the time to fulfill the president's wishes. In 1986 Scowcroft had been tapped to serve on the Tower Commission that investigated the Iran-Contra scandal, writing the section of the final report pertaining to reforms of the NSC system. Scowcroft concluded that sound national security decision-making required, in the words of Jane Holl Lute, "an established, inclusive, and deliberate process to allow the principals ... to provide the president with their frank advice." The national security adviser played an essential role "not only to oversee this process, but also to establish sound operating systems and secure the best possible expertise to support the president in foreign policy making."[55] To Scowcroft, the national security adviser had to be an "honest broker" of information, a label that is deceptively simplistic when one considers the immense strains placed on the managers of the foreign policy process in times of crisis and war.

Serving the president as an honest broker did not mean that the national security adviser and NSC staff were prohibited from offering their own independent recommendations to the president. Rather, the norm articulated in the Tower Commission report and embodied in the Bush administration was that *all* participants' views had to be given a fair shake.[56] This is easier said than done; Scowcroft knew that because of his proximity to Bush his views could carry extraordinary weight. To avoid putting his thumb on the scale, Scowcroft always offered his perspective only after he presented the views of the other principals.

Bush and Scowcroft created a system of strategic decision-making that has yet to be rivaled in its effectiveness in providing the president with a wide range of policy options and ensuring agency and departmental follow-through. In January 1989 the basic structure of the system was laid out in National Security Directive (NSD) 1. According to the document, foreign policy would be made by four hierarchically arranged committees. On the bottom were the policy coordinating committees (PCCs). Staffed by members of various departments at the assistant secretary level, the PCCs were responsible for developing national security policies for individual regions (e.g., East Asia) and functional areas (e.g., arms control). Above the PCCs was the Deputies Committee (DC), a body made up of the highest-ranking deputy secretaries responsible for policy in each department with a national security purview. Chaired by deputy national security adviser Robert Gates, the DC was originally tasked with monitoring the work of the NSC interagency process that was being carried out by the PCCs and for making further recommendations on the development of national security policy. The Principals Committee (PC) was chaired by Scowcroft and included all the senior advisers to the president but did not include Bush himself. Scowcroft was sensitive to the fact that time was the most precious of presidential commodities and the PC was designed as a forum intended to handle matters that did not need direct presidential intervention.[57] Sitting atop this structure was the National Security Council (NSC), the formal body for presidential consultation made up by the president, vice president, the secretaries of state and defense, director of central intelligence, chairman of the joint chiefs of staff, the president's chief of staff, and the national security adviser. When appropriate, the treasury secretary and attorney general would be invited to attend NSC meetings.[58]

On paper this structure held much promise, but it broke down in practice. In October 1989 the administration was caught flat-footed when an attempted coup was launched against the Panamanian leader Gen. Manuel Noriega. Unable to coordinate an effective response to the unfolding crisis to the south, Scowcroft saw that the structure he and Bush had devised contained no mechanism for managing international crises. On October 25, 1989, a supplement to NSD 1 was issued giving this responsibility to the DC.[59] With this change to the DC's mandate the committee was supercharged, emerging as the "engine of the policy process." The DC became the central forum for the development of medium- and long-term objectives of US policy that implicated all national security departments, oversight of the day-to-day functioning of the policy process, and the handling of international crises as they emerged.[60] It was, in other words, the central hub in the Bush administration's strategic decision-making system. As the DC's purview expanded, the salience of the PC and NSC diminished. Under Gates's leadership, the DC performed at such a high level of proficiency that there was little left for the PC to handle; whatever matters could not be dealt with by the DC necessitated Bush's intervention. Bush found formal NSC meetings to be unwieldy, moreover, and so an informal grouping was created. Called the Core Group, or Big 8, this body included Bush, Scowcroft, Baker, Cheney, Gates, Powell, White House Chief of Staff John Sununu, and Vice President Dan Quayle.[61]

In addition to Scowcroft's role as an honest broker, three norms guided the process of foreign policymaking in the Bush administration. The first norm pertained to access: all deputies had to have access to, and be fully empowered to speak on behalf of, their principals. Gates, for example, was given the title "assistant to the president," which meant that he had Bush's ear and was the only nonprincipal to attend Core Group meetings. Gates's ability to instantly gain an audience with the president enhanced his standing among his colleagues at the deputy level. "During one deputies' meeting," Gates recounted, "we really had a serious disagreement and I said, 'Well, I'll just find out what the President wants.' I left the meeting, went up, talked to Bush, came back down, said, 'Here's what we're going to do.' That kind of thing gets around." The other deputies had to have similar access to their principals as well.[62]

Due process was the second norm. Bush again set the tone by insisting that thorough intelligence and policy analysis inform every decision. The premium placed on high quality analysis pervaded the DC. Gates refused to allow DC meetings to devolve into bull sessions because each of the principals expected the committee to provide them with sound policy options based on extensive analysis. As Zelikow notes,

> One of the most singular characteristics of this group was that they were committed to analysis and they were disciplined about getting it. And that has all kinds of implications all the way down. If you have a deputies committee that says we're not going to discuss this issue until somebody's written a decent quality paper on this that's more than just a few bullet points, then that means the paper has to be tasked and drafted . . . when you're not making it up and when you insist on having that kind of analysis going in you get better policy.[63]

Quality control over the foreign policy process—the determination by Scowcroft and Gates to ensure that nothing fell through the cracks—was the third critical norm. Scowcroft understood that no matter how difficult it may be to reach a decision, making sure that the decision has, in fact, been executed in the intended time and manner is even more onerous. "Policy is really made by the outgoing cables from State and Defense," Scowcroft recalled. Knowing this, the national security adviser had his staff carefully monitor the daily outgoing cable traffic "to make sure that what was going out to the field hadn't been passed like that game of telephone with kids in a room."[64]

Combined, the structure of the Bush administration's strategic decision-making process and the norms that infused it resulted in an auspicious information flow pattern throughout the government. The president and senior advisers were afforded with a diversity of perspectives and proposals from across the national security bureaucracy. At the same time, information was widely and routinely shared among the national security organizations in the DC and PCCs, breaking down the barriers that can prevent effective collaboration at lower levels. Previous studies show that this type of information flow pattern has beneficial results in terms of the quality of strategic decision-making. Not only is a wide range of perspectives made available to senior leaders but the proposals submitted for consideration must run the gauntlet of intense interagency vetting. Further, senior leaders can ensure collaboration among the various national security organizations by monitoring the activities of their subordinate departments. As those departments share information with each other, they are more tightly knitted together in a system that rewards cooperation and punishes defection.[65]

This robust information flow pattern had an additional effect, institutionalizing President Bush's strategic beliefs in the decision-making process. The Bush-Scowcroft system enabled the president's goals to serve as the focal point orienting the policies and behaviors of the national security bureaucracy. Bush and Scowcroft were the only senior officials whose purview included all the domains of grand strategy: military, diplomatic, intelligence, and economic. The two men were empowered to drive the strategy-making process and prevent it from atrophying throughout the bureaucracy. All the administration's major strategic initiatives, Gates explained, "were sparked by either Bush or Brent [Scowcroft] and it was always the two of them pushing the rest of the administration, pushing Cheney and pushing Baker in particular." Continuing, Gates recalled that it fell to Scowcroft and him to translate "where the President wanted to go into an administration consensus in getting there."[66] Supported by Scowcroft and Gates, Bush was firmly at the center of the foreign policy process. Through this decision-making system, George Bush's strategic beliefs guided the development and implementation of American grand strategy.

George Bush came to office with a set of strategic beliefs about how the international system functioned, America's role in world affairs, the nature of the threats to US interests, the relative value of the instruments of national power, and the importance of information diversity. Bush believed the United States was a force for good in the world and had the capacity to lead its allies, partners, and would-be partners in the creation of a more secure, prosperous, and peaceful international environment. While that vision was bold, Bush's methods were cautious and disciplined. The world contained threats that had to be managed, and if necessary, confronted using all the tools of US statecraft. Bush believed that American security was enhanced when the country worked closely with others, preferably through international institutions. Yet, he did not see collective security mechanisms as a panacea. Rather, he believed that collective security could only function when it was supported by the military and economic might of the United States. To Bush's way of thinking, the United States was the only nation that could lead its friends and partners; America was first among equals. Because the threats to US interests were varied and often diffused, that leadership had to be steady and determined, predicated on policies that benefited from a wide range of information about the strategic environment. The practice of effective statecraft could only result from the robust analysis of intelligence and the careful matching of means to ends.

To transform these strategic beliefs into actual grand strategy, Bush needed an apparatus that provided him with high quality information originating from all the national security departments and agencies under him. He also needed his decision-making system to ensure that the departments acted in ways that fulfilled his policy agenda and not the narrow parochial interests that frequently motivate bureaucracies. To be sure, the high degree of collegiality among Bush's senior advisers was important to achieving these goals. More important, however, was the foreign policy process that he, Scowcroft, and Gates established early in his term. Through this system, Bush was able to fashion a bold grand strategy that would seek to end the Cold War and transform European politics on terms that were highly beneficial to the United States and to establish a new world order for the post–Cold War era. It is to that grand strategy that we now turn.

CHAPTER 2

The New World Order Grand Strategy, 1989–1990

George Bush's grand strategy for a new world order emerged early in his tenure, orienting US relations with a transforming Soviet Union and with four regions from 1989 to late 1991: Central and Eastern Europe, East Asia, Latin America, and the Middle East. Bush's approach prioritized objectives, was sensitive to the relationship between means and ends, and leveraged all instruments of statecraft. The New World Order grand strategy flowed directly from the president's strategic beliefs and was pursued coherently through the administration's interagency decision-making system.

Europe Whole and Free

The Bush administration maintained a Janus-faced approach to the changing international system. In certain respects, Bush and his top advisers placed a premium on caution and prudence. Bush, of course, himself applied the term "prudent" in describing his approach toward the Soviet Union because, initially, his administration harbored concerns that Ronald Reagan had embraced Mikhail Gorbachev too readily and recklessly.[1] In a landmark speech at the UN in September 1988, Gorbachev committed the Soviet Union to the principles of self-determination, the rule of law, and self-restraint in military affairs. Also at the UN, Soviet foreign minister Eduard Shevardnadze repudiated class struggle as a guiding principle of international relations. These sweeping declarations notwithstanding, Bush frustrated Gorbachev by slowing down the process of Soviet-American reconciliation. While Gorbachev was speaking the language of reform, Bush assessed that "the Soviets retain a very powerful military machine in the service of objectives which are still too often in conflict with ours."[2] Moscow had much left to prove before the new American president would consider it a full-fledged partner.

The Bush administration's caution regarding the unfolding events in Europe induced an interagency policy review process in the initial weeks of 1989. Substantively, this review process (known as "the pause" in America's engagement with Gorbachev) produced little in the way of innovative policy proposals. What the process did offer the administration was time to collect its thoughts and to consider how the United States could steal the momentum from Gorbachev and to steer the transformation in European security affairs in a direction more amenable to the administration. "I did not want to be seen as lagging behind Gorbachev with nit-picking, foot-dragging responses," Bush recalled, "yet I certainly did not want to make a foolish or short-sighted move either."[3]

The administration acted cautiously, but its aspirations were bold. As Bush's national security adviser Brent Scowcroft recounted, the president-elect told his top advisers that they "should dream big dreams ... We thought we should change our sights from managing the Cold War on the ground in Europe and stabilizing the situation to look beyond, to resolution of the basic issues."[4] It did not take long for the basic issues to come into focus, and the administration's strategy of resolving them was ambitious from the start.[5] The set of goals that would eventually be labeled "the new world order" was born in the early months of the Bush administration, as its principal actors recognized that fundamental changes were occurring in the world and that they augured opportunities for America that needed to be carefully fostered. If realized, these changes would amount to a new world order, but to get to that world, three historically ingrained assumptions about interstate relations had to be discarded.

The first was the division of Europe that the Cold War had reified. Bush insisted that for the Cold War to truly end, Europe must be "whole and free." In its earliest policy formulation, the administration insisted that Europe's political divisions had to be resolved on the basis of "Western values": free elections and markets, the respect for sovereignty and territorial integrity abroad, and the protection of human rights domestically.[6] With respect to the most important political division, Bush rejected the assumption, oft repeated by Gorbachev and Shevardnadze, that history had irrevocably determined that there should be two Germanies.[7] All European states would have to come to terms with the German people's national aspirations for unification, Bush insisted. To make that accommodation possible, Bush asserted from the beginning that unification would occur, that a unified and democratic Germany would be a full member of NATO, and that all Soviet forces on the territory of the former German Democratic Republic (GDR) would have to be withdrawn.[8]

Making the German question particularly difficult was a second historical legacy, one that had its roots not in the Cold War but in World War II: the assertion by both the Western allies and the Soviets of privileged rights of the victors. The notion that the Four Powers (Britain, France, the Soviet Union, and the United States) retained the right to dictate German domestic and foreign policies infused much of the debate over the prospects for unification.[9] Bush maintained that the Federal Republic of Germany (FRG) had proven its democratic and pacific bona fides in the decades since the end of the war and he rejected the notion that other powers had the right to restrict the principles of self-determination and sovereignty, especially when they emerged freely.[10] In place of victors' rights, Bush championed democratic sovereignty in his administration's diplomacy with America's allies and the Soviet Union.

The final legacy standing in the way of the new world order was the ideological conflict between the democratic capitalist West and communist East. Much of Bush's caution and prudence stemmed from the concern among administration officials that Gorbachev's New Thinking and perestroika could be rolled back if they were not fully embedded in democratic institutions. It was the institutionalization of political, economic, and military reforms that would be the true litmus tests of Soviet intentions, not the substance of the reform policies themselves—

no matter how welcomed they may have been.[11] Gorbachev's ability to lock in his sweeping reform agenda was critical to the durability of great power cooperation in international security affairs.

By April–May 1989, Washington settled on a set of strategic objectives for Europe. First, it would be the administration's policy to facilitate democratization in East Europe, an agenda that would add substance to the notion of a "Europe whole and free." Bush announced in an April 17 speech in Hamtramck, Michigan, the provision of foreign aid to countries like Poland that were undertaking political liberalization, as opposed to only economic liberalization. Aware of the risks inherent in the rapid changes taking place in Central and Eastern Europe (not the least of which was the fact that these states were members of the Warsaw Pact), Bush refused to give Poland and Hungary a blank check.[12] Furthermore, America's own economic circumstances (e.g., the need to rein in spending after years of Reagan-era budget deficits) limited Washington's ability to provide substantial aid to liberalizing states. "Our strategy for Eastern Europe was to reward moves toward liberalism. Reward meant aid of one kind or another," Scowcroft later explained. Yet, "there was no extra money, no emergency money possible. It was the worst time in the world to implement the policy we had."[13] The United States would assist these states, but Bush insisted they would have to carry much of the burden themselves.[14] At the G7 meeting in Paris in mid-July 1989, an aid package came together. Significantly, economic and food aid destined for Eastern Bloc countries would be coordinated by the European Community. As Kristina Spohr explains, this multilateral approach lifted "Western engagement with Eastern Europe out of the superpower domain, spread the burden and [made] possible a larger, more synchronized and less competitive Western effort." Multilateral aid to Eastern Europe also made American policy less threatening to the Soviets, thereby reducing the chances of a Kremlin-sponsored crackdown on the nascent reform movements.[15]

Second, Bush decided to make German unification a cornerstone of America's policy toward Europe. Not only was he the furthest ahead in his administration on the question of reunification, but Bush was alone among Western leaders on the issue. On May 31 in Mainz, Germany, Bush declared, "I will continue to do all I can to help open the closed societies of the East. We seek self-determination for all of Germany and all of Eastern Europe.... [T]he world has waited long enough."[16] Yet, German reunification entailed the clash of two principles that Bush sought to uphold. First, German unity reflected the will of millions of German citizens, on both sides of the now rusting Iron Curtain, to live together in a single political community. How that entity would form and what it would ultimately look like were, for Bush, matters that should be left to Germans to decide. As such, Bush insisted that outside powers not interfere with the political aspirations that the German leadership was espousing. The call of unification was a manifestation of the FRG's democratic sovereign rights that had to be respected. The principle of democratic sovereign rights would eventually apply to the GDR when it held truly free elections in March 1990, the results of which ended control of the GDR by the Social Democrats.

The prospect of a united Germany, however, had profound security implications for all European powers. Cognizant of this reality, the second principle that Bush was determined to uphold was that America would remain the leading Western power in Europe. The transformations under way on the continent had the potential to displace the United States, especially if new institutions replaced NATO as the central pillar in Europe's security architecture. As the drive for unification intensified, the Bush administration made the critical decision to insist that a unified Germany would be a fully committed member of the North Atlantic alliance. In early November, Francis Fukuyama, then a member of the State Department's Policy Planning Staff, proposed that US policy on unification be oriented on four points, the second of which was the most critical: (1) that German unification be based on self-determination, (2) that a united Germany be a full member of NATO, (3) that unification be handled in a stepwise and deliberate fashion, and (4) that Germany's borders with its neighbors remain fixed.[17] In early December, Bush secured allied support for these points at a NATO summit in Brussels. In the process, NATO's relevance was enhanced and Washington's leadership position in NATO was strengthened.[18]

Washington understood that NATO membership for a united Germany would likely be perceived by Kremlin as its worst nightmare.[19] By then, however, the Bush administration was well into its effort to fundamentally reorient the Soviet-American relationship in ways that were more cooperative but also decisively on America's terms. The third objective to emerge in the first months of 1989 was to move "beyond containment" by incentivizing liberalization in the Soviet Union itself with the goal of bringing it into the democratic capitalist international system. Written shortly after the official security review process ended, National Security Directive (NSD)-23 held that the USSR's new relationship with the United States had to be "earned through the demilitarization of Soviet foreign policy and reinforced by behavior consistent with the principles of world order to which the Soviet Union subscribed in 1945 but has repeatedly violated since."[20] As Bush explained in his speech to the graduating class at Texas A&M University on May 12, 1989, America's new policy toward the Soviet Union would grasp the "precious opportunity" that "forty years of perseverance have brought us.... The United States now has as its goal much more than containing Soviet expansionism. We seek the integration of the Soviet Union into the community of nations."[21]

The United States would seek "fundamental alterations in Soviet military force structure, institutions, and practices which can only be reversed at great cost, economically and politically, to the Soviet Union." Washington's terms for a new cooperative relationship included: a smaller and less threateningly deployed Soviet force posture, the repudiation of class conflict as the source of international tension, the renunciation of the Brezhnev Doctrine and the support for the territorial integrity of all states, and the "demilitarization of Soviet foreign policy in other regions of the world and serious participation in efforts to ameliorate conflict, including bringing pressure to bear on Soviet clients who do not recognize the legitimate security interests of their neighbors." Recognizing that the achievement of these objectives would be difficult, requiring a surfeit of American "patience and creativity," NSD-23 argued that Washington must pressure Moscow at every step to live up to the standards that it was now advocating through perestroika. This pressure would matter most immediately in East-Central Europe, where the United States was encouraging fundamental political and economic reform "so that states in that region may once again be productive members of a prosperous, peaceful, and democratic Europe, whole and free from fear of Soviet intervention."[22]

Pressuring Gorbachev to live up to the standards of perestroika would matter outside Europe as well. Presaging Soviet-American cooperation in the Persian Gulf War, NSD-23 directed Secretary of State James Baker to "consider the most appropriate ways to engage the Soviets in discussions on resolving regional conflicts and eliminating threatening Soviet positions of influence around the world."[23] Bush's determination to work with the Soviets was genuine. "Our policy is to seize every—and I mean every—opportunity to build a better, more stable relationship with the Soviet Union," Bush stated on May 24 at the US Coast Guard Academy. While it remained the mission of the United States to "defend American interests in light of the enduring reality of Soviet military power ... there's an opportunity before us to shape a new world."[24]

Thus, by no later than May 1989—months before the fall of the Berlin Wall—the Bush administration had established an ambitious strategy for Europe. America would seek to create a Europe whole and free and to move beyond containment with the Soviet Union. Specifically, the United States would encourage democracy in Central and Eastern Europe, push for the unification of Germany under the condition that the new state would be a full member of NATO (and retain the FRG's commitments to other European institutions, including the European Community), and grasp every opportunity to build a cooperative relationship with a politically liberalized Soviet Union that embraced the principles of the democratic-capitalist international order.[25] In laying out this agenda to the Berlin Press Club in December, Baker envisioned the United States promoting "a new Atlanticism," from which a new Europe would be born.[26]

The fundamental strategic challenge in 1989-1990, the management of the linkages among these objectives, was daunting. To convince the German people that they would be welcomed as full members of the Western security alliance, the United States needed its European allies to align with German national aspirations. This would prove difficult because Paris and London viewed a unified Germany as a likely security challenge. To assuage those allies' security fears, a united Germany needed to be a full member of NATO. The problem here was that Helmut Kohl, at the time chancellor of the FRG and soon to become chancellor of a united Germany, had to be persuaded to stand resolutely in favor of the new Germany's membership in the Western alliance. Kohl, however, was reticent to embrace NATO membership for fear that the Kremlin would block unification due to its own security concerns.[27] Thus, NATO membership for Germany had to be accepted by Moscow; accordingly, Bush recognized that the Soviets needed convincing that their complete capitulation on this issue would amount to a security boon. This was a difficult sell because Washington also saw German membership in NATO as a path toward the reduction and restructuring of Soviet conventional forces in Europe. With the Soviet forces out of the territory of the former GDR—the only conceivable outcome with Germany's full accession to NATO—a critical source of instability in Europe would be dealt with.[28] Furthermore, that instability was the principal obstacle to democratization of Central and East European countries. Only with broad acceptance of democratic values could Europe's divisions be bridged. In short, each of Washington's strategic objectives were linked, but none of them was easy to realize.

Central to Washington's strategy was the recognition that while structural change presented opportunities for America's interests in Europe, violence could erupt and progress could be quickly reversed. To protect America's position, Bush was committed to retaining the US military presence in Europe. The American forces forward deployed in Europe served as a vital security guarantee to Western allies. Maintaining a strong military presence also served as critical ballast to the Soviet military, a powerful reminder to the Kremlin that its use of force—even in Eastern Europe—would not be free of risk and cost.[29] As the dominant military power in Western Europe, moreover, the United States enjoyed significant leverage in NATO, influence that was necessary for achieving its complex set of objectives. Thus, in the 1989–1990 period the Bush administration viewed military power as a vital backstop to American diplomacy.

The most important component of Washington's diplomatic approach was retaining its leadership in the Western security alliance.

From that position, Washington could work to ensure that the political transformations in Europe occurred on terms acceptable to America.[30] As Bush noted in his diary on February 24, "I think we have a disproportionate role [in NATO] for stability [in Europe]." America's ability to provide stability for Europe was, for Bush, critical at this moment in history. Reflecting on the broad challenges confronting the United States, Bush continued:

> Who's the enemy? I keep getting asked that. It's apathy; it's the inability to predict accurately; it's dramatic changes that can't be foreseen; and its events that can't be predicted like the Iran-Iraq war.... [T]here are all kinds of events that we can't foresee that require a strong NATO, and there's all kinds of potential instability that requires a strong U.S. presence.[31]

Bush understood that he had two principal alliance leadership tasks: overcoming the preferences of the core states—primarily Britain, but also France—to consider the "German question" as a matter of the Four Powers' joint purview and ensconcing a unified Germany into existing regional political and military institutions. At the same time, Bush's view was that it was up to the two German states to determine the content and timing of German unification. For example, on November 18, 1989, Helmut Kohl delivered a speech to the Bundestag that laid out a ten-point plan for achieving unification. This presentation was the first comprehensive statement of Kohl's vision for unification, and it came as a great surprise to everyone in Europe—but not to Bush, with whom Kohl shared an advance copy.[32] Washington played no role in drafting the speech, and despite Baker's frustration that Kohl did not insist on a united Germany's unconditional membership in NATO, the Bush administration backed the chancellor's play.[33]

The speech received a chilly reception in London, Paris, and Moscow, however. To blunt criticisms and prevent the anticipated obstruction from the FRG's neighbors, Bush mounted a strong defense of the ten-point plan at the December 4 NATO summit in Brussels. Reminding the assembled heads of state that America and NATO had long supported the notion of a unified Germany, Bush stated that "unification should occur in the context of Germany's continued commitment to NATO and an increasingly integrated European Community, and with due regard for the legal role and responsibilities of Allied powers." Unification should occur, moreover, in a way that was "peaceful, gradual, and part of a step-by-step process," just as Kohl's ten-point plan envisioned. Finally, Bush declared that "an end to the unnatural division of Europe, and of Germany, must proceed in accordance with and be based upon the values that are becoming universal ideals, as all the countries of Europe become part of a commonwealth of free nations."[34]

With powerful backing from Bush, Kohl's plan would proceed in the face of weakened opposition from the FRG's Western neighbors.[35] By couching German unification in NATO and the EC, Bush addressed, but did not eradicate, serious security and political concerns in London and Paris. To further clear the path toward unification, Washington imposed an alternative multilateral process: the "Two Plus Four Power" formula. Originating in the State Department, the 2+4 process envisioned the FRG and GDR alone determining the details of unification, while granting the four victorious powers the role of overseeing the external implications of unification.[36] Critical to the 2+4 was the assumption that unification *would* occur; the arrangement would not be a debating forum on the merits of German unity. In devising this process, officials in the State Department recognized that the Soviets, British, and French had to be included in the most important diplomatic issue in the postwar era.[37] As one of the Four Powers, moreover, the United States would be well-positioned to prevent separate German-Soviet agreements and to ensure that the democratic sovereign rights of the two Germanies were respected.[38]

The ten-point plan that Kohl laid out in November 1989 quickly succumbed to events. Key to that plan was a viable government in the GDR that would cooperate in a gradual and managed political process. By February 1990, however, the East German government had effectively collapsed. In response, Kohl charted a new path for unification that entailed the FRG's direct absorption of the GDR by invoking Article 23 of the Basic Law that allowed other portions of Germany to simply join the FRG.[39] For this plan to work, Kohl would need East German citizens to vote the ruling East German Social Democrats out of office, which occurred on March 18. In briefing Bush on his new plan at Camp David on February 24, Kohl again found the American president supportive of his plan for rapid unification.[40] Kohl accepted Bush's argument that American forces should remain in Germany, that Soviet forces would have to leave the territory of the former GDR, and that a unified Germany would be a full member of NATO.[41]

Beyond Containment

Moving beyond containment with the Soviet Union—to reach a cooperative relationship with the Kremlin and bring it into the Western order—required the amelioration of the ideological competition that characterized the Cold War. Only when the Soviet Union demonstrated behavior consistent with the rhetoric of perestroika, Bush concluded, could a new world based on extensive great power cooperation be achieved. To test Gorbachev's sincerity, on January 31, 1990, Bush called for dramatic reductions in Soviet and American troop levels in Central and Eastern Europe, specifically to 195,000 on each side. In proposing equality, Washington's goal was, as Baker explained, to turn "a Soviet advantage in conventional forces into a disadvantage."[42] For the secretary of state, the Conventional Forces in Europe (CFE) proposal was a means of reducing a source of Soviet strategic advantage on the ground.[43] For Bush and Scowcroft, the CFE initiative was intended to test Gorbachev's intentions. Bush's proposal went further than anything Gorbachev proffered, and the president reasoned that if the Soviet leader was sincere in his vision of a "common European home," then he would have to cooperate with the United States on the core issue dividing the continent.[44]

In truth, Bush hoped Gorbachev was sincere. During his first meeting with Gorbachev at Malta in December 1989, Bush told the Soviet leader that "the world would be a better place if *perestroika* succeeds."[45] The meeting in Malta was of crucial importance to both sides. Gorbachev learned that the Americans were committed to expanding superpower cooperation at a critical time. Most significantly, Bush proposed an economic package that Gorbachev's foreign policy adviser Anatoly Chernyaev understood as being a "commitment to give economic support to perestroika, to our reforms." For his part, Bush saw that Gorbachev was attempting to transform Soviet foreign policy; at the same time, Gorbachev conveyed the message that an American triumphalist attitude would hinder his efforts. Recognizing the significance of this point, Bush replied, "We have not responded with flamboyance or arrogance that would complicate USSR relations.... I have conducted myself in ways not to complicate your life. That's why I have not jumped up and down on the Berlin Wall."[46] Turning to the issue of German unification, while insisting that "there are two German states, this was the decision of history," Gorbachev nevertheless stated his acceptance of Washington's strong influence and engagement in Europe. Furthermore, Gorbachev agreed that all states should be free to choose their own political and economic systems. Finally, the Soviet leader chafed at the notion that the division of Europe had to be settled on the basis of "Western values." Clarifying what he meant by the term, Baker stressed the importance of openness and pluralism and offered an alternative formulation: "democratic values." Gorbachev agreed with Baker's phrasing, noting, "They are our values, too."[47]

While the Malta summit provided a significant boost to Soviet-American trust, the hard task of convincing the Kremlin to accept German unification under NATO auspices remained.[48] The sense of insecurity that the Soviets would experience if the central pillar in their satellite system was folded into the American-led alliance needed to be overcome. State Department officials concluded that a diplomatic mechanism to enhance transparency and ensure Soviet buy-in was required. The 2+4 forum offered much in the way of assurances to the Kremlin regarding the West's intentions while at the same time paving the way for a rapid conclusion of the unification process. The problem was that, under this formulation, the Soviets retained a veto that they would likely use if they did not agree on the merits of a united Germany within NATO.[49]

As of May 31, 1990, Gorbachev had steadfastly refused to countenance NATO membership for Germany. Security assurances embodied in the 2+4 brought the Soviets along, but they were not enough: the road to unification on American terms still went through Moscow. At the Washington Summit, Bush noted to Gorbachev that the Helsinki Final Act provided that all states had the right to choose their alliances. "To me," Bush recalled, "that meant Germany should be able to decide for itself what it wanted. Did he agree?" Surprisingly, Gorbachev did. Clarifying, Bush posed the issue baldly: "We support a united Germany in NATO. If they don't want in, we will respect that." Again, Gorbachev consented.[50]

Gorbachev's acquiescence on this critical issue to Soviet national security stemmed from several reinforcing factors. Zelikow and Rice point to two principal issues: the inability of Gorbachev to move Bush from his position regarding NATO despite his many attempts to do so, and the soundness of Bush's appeal to democratic self-determination. "Gorbachev had often adopted the rhetoric of free choice and national self-determination. So when Bush struck the wall of resistance from this new angle, it suddenly cracked."[51] To these explanations, another should be added: Bush's consistency in offering Gorbachev opportunities to capitulate gracefully. As former State Department official Robert Zoellick argued, Bush "offered Gorbachev respect, not concessions that weakened the strength of the United States or NATO. . . . Bush and Baker respected their counterparts' dignity and, within the limits of prudence, assisted them."[52] By appealing to the logic of perestroika and by demonstrating over time that he would be the valuable partner the Soviet leader needed, Bush helped Gorbachev to concede—at least to Bush, but not yet publicly—to a unified Germany within NATO.

Some contend that Gorbachev was induced to concede to the prospect of a united Germany in NATO by the supposed assurance Baker gave to Gorbachev and Shevardnadze on February 9 that "NATO's jurisdiction would not shift one inch eastward from its present position."[53] Visiting Gorbachev in Moscow shortly after Baker departed, Kohl repeated Baker's phrasing to the general secretary. Whereas Baker's proposition was cast in hypothetical terms, Kohl's was more emphatic. It would be a mistake, however, to conclude that Baker's and Kohl's statements concerning NATO's future were central to Gorbachev's agreement that Germany had the right to choose whether to join the Atlantic alliance. In the near term, Bush was intent on avoiding limitations on NATO forces in the territory of the former East Germany. Nor did he support a priori restrictions on NATO's longer-term eastward expansion. As such, the administration quickly signaled that it was not willing to countenance any restrictions on Germany's future status in NATO, and Baker never again employed the "not one inch" formulation. To the contrary, Baker followed Bush's line that NATO would expand eastward by creating a special status for East German territory, a gesture that allowed Gorbachev to save some face.[54] Meanwhile, Hungary, Czechoslovakia, and Poland were not hiding their desires for NATO membership, or barring that, a close association with the alliance. Bush neither endorsed the Visegrád states' aspirations, nor did he dispel them publicly. Ultimately, NATO's eastward expansion was not a burning concern for Gorbachev, who never pressed his Western counterparts to have their assurances codified. As the future foreign minister of Russia Yevgeny Primakov noted ruefully, "With great regret, one has to conclude that the assurances by the Western leaders were not put into a treaty or legal form. However, we have every reason to believe that at that time it could have been done."[55]

Gorbachev did need financial and security assistance, however, and Bush was willing to help as best he could. At their meeting at Camp David, Kohl told Bush that he believed Gorbachev's acquiescence could be purchased. "This may end up as a matter of cash," Kohl noted. "They need money." To this Bush responded, "You have deep pockets."[56] Kohl ultimately pledged DM 12 billion to facilitate the withdrawal of Soviet Army forces from the territory of the DRG and another DM 3 billion of interest-free credits—a lifeline to the Soviet economy, and to Gorbachev.[57]

Assistance on the security front came in the form of changes made to NATO's mission and doctrine, a transformation that reduced the threat confronting the Soviet Union and bolstered Gorbachev's domestic position at a critical moment. On May 4, 1990, Bush outlined his ideas for NATO's future role in Europe, touching on the issues of conventional forces levels, the role of nuclear weapons deployed on the continent, and the ways that the Conference on Security and Cooperation in Europe (CSCE) could augment NATO by protecting democratic values in the new era.[58] Transforming NATO was no trivial matter. To Bush, Baker, and Scowcroft, a more politically oriented NATO, with conventional force levels determined by a future CFE treaty, would reduce the security pressure on the Soviets, ensure the organization's existence, and bolster US leadership in Europe. In calling for a new NATO, Bush was able to counter proposals coming from Moscow and Paris to make the CSCE the principal security institution in Europe. Formed in 1975 as part of the Helsinki Final Act, the CSCE had a broad remit and was the only institution that included all European states from the West and East.[59] Administration officials believed Gorbachev's call for the establishment of a system of collective security under CSCE auspices would ultimately reduce American influence in European security affairs.[60] Bush's proposal to associate NATO with the CSCE offered Eastern Bloc states a seat at the table while preserving NATO as the central organization for European security.[61]

On July 5 at the NATO summit in London, the alliance agreed to enhance its political mission and abandon its military doctrine of forward defense, signaled that the decision to use nuclear weapons would be made only as a last resort, and proposed strengthening the CSCE in important, yet still circumscribed, ways. A few days later, Gorbachev was reelected as the Soviet Union's general secretary at the Twenty-Eighth Party Congress. After a meeting with Kohl in Stavropol on July 14, Gorbachev signaled publicly for the first time that a united Germany would likely be a NATO member state. Briefing Bush after the meeting, Kohl stated that Gorbachev acknowledged the importance of NATO's declaration in enabling him to officially concede on this critical point.[62]

Finally, in November 1990, the CFE treaty was signed, an arms control agreement that, as Zelikow and Rice explain, "reduced and limited the conventional armed forces of at least twenty-three countries in Europe from the Atlantic to the Urals (every then-member of the NATO and Warsaw Pact alliances)."[63] The CFE treaty was the most ambitious arms control agreement in history, entailing steep cuts in the two bloc's forces. As Baker well understood, these reductions were asymmetrical, with the heavier burden falling on the Soviets—a source of resentment among many Soviet military officers. For Bush, the CFE treaty was of monumental importance, leading him to declare that its signing "signals the new world order that is emerging."[64]

By summer 1990 the Bush administration's strategy toward Europe and the Soviet Union had been developed and implemented. The pillars of that strategy are found in Bush's speeches in Hamtramck and Mainz, which laid out the two objectives of promoting democracy in

Central-East Europe and German unification; the administration's diplomacy at the NATO summit, which laid the ground for full NATO membership of a united Germany; and NSD-23, which made it American policy to incentivize Soviet reforms such that the USSR could be a partner to the United States in addressing common threats in the emerging world order. While these objectives may not have been novel, they were nevertheless ambitious and difficult to achieve.[65] Bush's strategy had played a significant role in ending Europe's political and military divisions and in dramatically improving Soviet-American relations on terms established by Washington.[66]

Managing Threats to America's Objectives: Tactics and Strategy

Bush administration officials understood that while the international system was evolving in a genuinely positive direction, threats to America's objectives loomed. Among more immediate concerns was the possible undoing of Gorbachev's reform process. As Scowcroft later recounted, "One of the things I watched closely was for indications that Gorbachev was running into deep trouble and perhaps facing a coup or something like that."[67] In the main, however, threats to the emerging new world order could not be identified precisely. As Jeffrey Engel notes, Bush understood that "change did not have to turn out for the best.... Because he longed to extend the sphere of American-led democracy, bringing new areas under the American orbit of stability, Bush feared volatility most of all."[68] Volatility, Bush recognized, could originate from the very processes that he was championing—political and economic liberalization and the end of Soviet control over its clients around the world.[69] Instability was an intrinsic feature of a system in flux. The fundamental challenge for the United States was to act in ways that fostered positive developments, while containing and, if possible, eradicating the disruptive forces to those trends.

The administration adopted a combination of tactical and strategic responses to manage this new amorphous threat environment. Bush's prudential policies and diplomatic style constituted the tactical approach. As detailed above, Bush foreswore opportunities to "jump up and down on the Berlin Wall" or to rhetorically invoke America's "victory" in the Cold War. As Scowcroft suggested, moreover, the substance of Washington's policies had to be keyed to events in the Soviet Union, a realization that pressing Gorbachev too hard and too fast would likely redound negatively on Bush's ultimate objectives. In this sense, the administration's deft diplomacy and Bush's repeated appeals to "prudence" were tactical moves to foster liberalization and push Gorbachev along, but at a pace that would neither stymie reform nor trigger political backlash.[70]

Much less appreciated in the literature are the strategic responses the Bush administration adopted to cope with uncertainty, instability, and potential volatility in the new international system. The effort to bolster US leadership in a newly transformed NATO was one strategic approach taken with this in mind. So too was the way Bush, Baker, and Scowcroft prioritized the world's regions and crafted policies that enabled administration officials to concentrate on, and devote resources to, their primary area of concern. George Bush's initial grand strategy privileged Europe over Asia, Latin America, and the Middle East. US foreign policies toward those regions were indeed cautious, seeking stability and predictability above all else.

Whereas, at the start of his term, the forty-first president was intent on pressing pause on Soviet-American rapprochement, Bush showed no such hesitancy toward China. After a decade of economic reform, China was emerging as a powerful actor in the world economy. Bush toyed with the idea of bringing China into a "Trans-Pacific Partnership," a regionwide economic arrangement that would, in addition to its economic benefits, help to spur political liberalization that the Chinese Communist Party under Deng Xiaoping had thus far prevented. Yet, scant policy ideas came from this concept. Bush, like many others at the time and since, believed that China's economic liberalization would inevitably generate political reforms.[71] For the time being, maintaining a stable relationship with the PRC, not introducing sweeping initiatives, was Bush's primary objective.

Two factors challenged Bush's goal of sustaining a strong working relationship with China. The first, and more general, development was that the waning of the Cold War upended the rationale of the Nixon-era policy toward China, which sought to leverage Beijing as a counterweight to Moscow.⁷² With the foundation of America's strategic approach to China eroding, Bush understood that a more China-centric China policy was needed, involving a new rationale for the relationship at a time when the Soviets were keen to initiate their own outreach to the PRC.⁷³ The issue was whether China under an aging Deng would be willing to maintain its policies of economic liberalization and its relationship with the United States.

The second development was the Tiananmen massacre that occurred in June 1989. Coming on the heels of the president's speeches on democracy promotion in Central-East Europe and German unification, many in the United States expected Bush to take a firm stand against China's leaders who responded to the pro-democracy protests by killing thousands of Chinese citizens. As a signal of US displeasure, the administration suspended—temporarily—senior-level exchanges, implemented financial and economic sanctions, and curtailed military sales to China. Yet, these policy responses were to a considerable extent adopted to mollify Democratic leaders in the US Congress who lambasted Bush's tepid response to the events.⁷⁴ In Bush's view, however, a strongly principled response would do little to improve the prospects of political liberalization in China. Much more could be gained by attempting to preserve the working relationship between the two countries.⁷⁵ As such, Bush kept the door open for diplomacy with the PRC.⁷⁶ And while the president was being pressured to respond to Tiananmen by elevating human rights in America's China policy, investment, student exchanges, and governmental visits to China were resumed by 1991. In selecting this course, as one analyst has put it, "the president's instinct was to preserve as much of the U.S.-China relationship as possible, prioritizing geostrategic and personal leadership ties over human rights concerns."⁷⁷ Further, as Scowcroft recalled, the administration saw "that the regime was in a panic" and was worried that there was "greater internal instability in China that we had to be very careful about."⁷⁸ Recognizing that a complete rupture with Beijing over Tiananmen would distract Washington from its ultimate grand strategic objectives in Europe, the Bush administration sought managed predictability in US-Chinese relations in order to cordon off the PRC as a source of instability and volatility.

Baker knew that US-Soviet relations and the management of the end of the Cold War in Europe would require a substantial amount of his attention. The secretary of state could ill afford to be drawn into crises in areas that were of peripheral concern to the administration. During the presidential transition period, Baker sought counsel from all the living secretaries of state. Recalling their advice, Baker noted many of them warned him "to be careful of the Arab-Israeli dispute; it's sort of a graveyard for Secretaries of State."[79] At the same time, Baker knew that the Middle East was a strategically important region and that the Arab-Israeli peace process was a fixture of American domestic politics. "I could either manage the issue or let it manage me," Baker concluded. "Like it or not, I didn't have the luxury of totally ignoring it." In its dealings with the two sides, the Bush administration adopted a "moderately activist policy," one that avoided the type of shuttle diplomacy made famous by Henry Kissinger.[80] Prior to the Persian Gulf War, US diplomats remained engaged with political affairs in the Middle East, but in a way that enabled them to focus on more strategically pressing matters in Europe.

Whereas Baker refused to be drawn into an intractable situation in the Middle East, from his first days in office he was determined to resolve a conflict closer to home that was consuming US domestic politics, the civil war in Nicaragua—a bloody, four-year-long conflict between the Moscow-backed Sandinista regime and the Contra rebels. Not only was the war a source of regional instability but it was a bone of partisan contention in the United States. Baker understood that bipartisan congressional support for US diplomacy to Eastern Europe and the Soviet Union would be essential in the coming months. He thus spearheaded an effort to get the Nicaraguan conflict out of US domestic politics. Knowing that Congress would not support any additional military assistance to the Contras, Baker proposed a humanitarian aid package to the rebels that would permit them to survive until the Nicaraguan elections scheduled for February 1990, at which time Washington would recognize whichever side emerged victorious. Baker's plan was criticized by Republicans and Democrats alike, yet it charted a middle course that minimally satisfied both parties.[81] Praising the Bipartisan Accord on Central America, Bush declared on March 14, 1989, "Today, for the first time in many years, the President and Congress, the Democratic and Republican leadership in the House and Senate, are speaking with one voice about Central America."[82] Through their negotiations with congressional leaders, Bush and Baker were able to end a significant partisan dispute over US foreign policy that threatened to derail more strategically important issues on the administration's agenda.

The bipartisan agreement did much to cordon off Central America as a source of instability in the first half of 1989. At the end of that year, however, America's attention again turned to the region, this time in more dramatic fashion. After a period of increasing governmental corruption, civil unrest, and state-sponsored violence in Panama, Bush decided to seek the ouster of Panamanian leader Gen. Manuel Noriega. Noriega, whose government declared on December 17 that a state of war existed with the United States, commanded the Panama Defense Force (PDF), an organization that had become extensively involved in the transshipment of drugs originating from Colombia. When the PDF shot three US servicemen, killing one, Bush ordered an invasion to overthrow the authoritarian regime, restore stability to the country and the vital Panama Canal Zone, and set conditions for a restoration of Panamanian democracy. US military operations, while limited in scale, were nonetheless overwhelming and quickly neutralized the PDF. Although Bush viewed Noriega and the PDF as threats to US interests, the operation was not without risk. As William Martel explains, "Any outcome that produced less than a total defeat of the PDF would preserve Noriega's rule, perpetuate authoritarian rule in Panama, unleash an insurgency, and weaken U.S. credibility."[83] In the end, the war lasted only a few hours and demonstrated that the United States could use military force effectively when its political and military objectives were clear and when it brought to bear a force of sufficient size to overwhelm the opposition. Operation Just Cause showed that while Europe and Soviet affairs were the most important grand strategic issues for the Bush administration, the American military could effectively handle threats to US interests elsewhere.

The Bush administration's New World Order grand strategy had been developed and implemented by summer 1989. The strategy sought to create a "Europe whole and free" and to move "beyond containment" of the Soviet Union. Specifically, Bush sought to foster democracy and market economies in Central and Eastern Europe, to end the political division of Europe by supporting Germain unification on the condition that the newly united country be a full NATO member, and to integrate a reforming Soviet Union into the Western political-economic order. To achieve these objectives, Bush and his team would leverage all the instruments of national power. Diplomatic efforts were in the foreground as Bush and Baker forged a partnership with Gorbachev and worked to uphold Germany's democratic sovereign rights, all the while making the expression of those rights—unification—acceptable to Germany's neighbors. Through a combination of bilateral and multilateral initiatives, the Bush administration created mechanisms that transformed Europe and superpower relations in ways that satisfied the minimal security requirements of all parties. These included the 2+4 forum, the transformation of NATO, the bridging of NATO and the CSCE, and the CFE initiative. Militarily, Bush ensured that the United States would retain a sizable presence in Europe, but in a way that reduced the threat to the Soviet Union. America provided economic assistance to foster liberalization in former Eastern Bloc states and backed EC efforts to provide much more aid.

Threats to these initiatives were understood to be uncertainty, instability, and volatility—amorphous but still disruptive forces endemic to the very processes that Washington was supporting. Bush, Baker, and Scowcroft devised tactical and strategic responses to manage these threats. Tactically, the administration's diplomacy was prudent to the core, carefully conducted so as not to move too quickly, or to come off as arrogant and triumphalist. Strategically, Bush sought to perpetuate US leadership in Europe and to cordon off instability and volatility emanating from other regions in the world. Finally, Bush believed that deep cooperation among nations would preserve peace and enhance prosperity. Bush's grand strategy was less costly than one premised on US primacy, but the reduction in up-front costs came with risk, specifically that America's most import partners would, for their own reasons, spurn cooperation with the United States as they sought to enhance their own security and influence in a changing international system.

The New World Order grand strategy was the product of Bush's strategic beliefs. As discussed in the chapter 1, Bush believed that the United States was most secure when it was able to exert strong leadership to forge deep cooperation among states. Both elements—leadership and cooperation—were evident in Bush's strategic approach. Cooperation was essential to the long-run stability of the international system. Although in 1989–1990 the system was anything but stable, it was moving in a direction amenable to US interests and values. Bush believed that multilateral consensus was the surest way to secure those gains over the long haul. But to forge cooperation, America could not afford to have its influence diluted. It was for this reason that Bush refused an alternative security architecture based on collective security through the CSCE, a concept supported by Gorbachev and Mitterrand. While the cooperative aspect of this scheme was enticing, American influence would be dramatically reduced if the CSCE replaced NATO as the principal organization responsible for European security. Bush was committed to multilateral security arrangements, but only if the United States was the first among equals. Critically for Bush, American leadership did not amount to American fiat; leadership meant listening to other leaders, taking their concerns seriously, and then forging solutions with them to resolve common problems. In dealing with leaders of other states, Bush (and Baker) evinced strategic empathy, a sense of what others needed, and a determination to work with them to craft durable solutions that would, in the end, satisfy US interests. Finally, Bush was attuned to the sheer complexity of the environment in which he operated and appreciated that complexity breeds instability. Bush was never content to rely on one source of information, nor did he ever feel that he knew enough. Inattention to detail could ruin the best conceived plans. Nor did Bush think that America's objectives could be secured through one instrument of power. Deft, mutually reinforcing combinations of military, economic, and diplomatic tools were essential to achieving America's grand strategic objectives.

Bush's strategic beliefs were well-suited for the international environment of 1989–1990. But not all members of the administration shared the president's perspectives. Secretary of Defense Cheney, along with others in the Pentagon, were far less inclined to forge a cooperative relationship with Gorbachev.[84] In fact, the DOD took steps to obstruct key elements of Bush's strategy. For example, in an April 29, 1989, CNN interview, Cheney expressed doubts about Gorbachev's chances of success in reforming Soviet foreign policy. Upon learning that Cheney had directly contradicted the administration's position, Baker was incensed, telling the secretary, "Cheney, you're off the reservation." Not content with Cheney's promise that it "won't happen again," Baker told Bush and Scowcroft that the White House should publicly distance itself from Cheney's comments. "Dump on Dick with all possible alacrity," Baker urged; and the White House did, with Bush going so far as to issue a statement expressing the most support for perestroika he had given up to that point.[85] More significant was the DOD's resistance to Bush's efforts to design and implement a sweeping CFE treaty. The Pentagon's position was "No. We should not move a man now. We will demoralize Europe," Scowcroft recalled. Cheney objected that US force reductions would "unhinge the Alliance" and that the "British and French would go crazy."[86] In the end, the CFE proposal was drafted not by the DOD but in the White House by the NSC staff.[87]

Bureaucratic resistance to initiatives sponsored by senior officials is common. Still, no president wants to have his or her initiatives obstructed by their own senior advisers. At stake is the coherent implementation of strategy. While the Bush administration stands as the most effective in modern history at ensuring interagency cooperation in foreign policy, that does not mean it was always smooth sailing. "Cheney was much less open, in giving NSC staffers access to their counterparts, than State was," Scowcroft noted. "Cheney wanted things to come through his office—which meant that much of the intelligence that I otherwise would have gotten, I didn't get. . . . I could find out anything I wanted, but I had to know what I wanted to get."[88] Fortunately for Bush, Scowcroft usually knew exactly what he wanted to get. Scowcroft and Gates had the responsibility of translating the president's strategic beliefs into a coherent grand strategy. Their success resulted from their effective management of Bush's system of strategic decision-making. That system provided the president and his senior advisers with a diversity of information and enforced collaboration among departments and agencies, even when collaboration wasn't welcomed.

In the summer of 1990, the primary contours of the New World Order grand strategy were in place. Yet, a key component of that strategy—situating great power cooperation in the United Nations—had yet to be devised. More than anything else, Saddam Hussein's invasion of Kuwait would enable the administration to add the missing piece, to elevate a strategy focused primarily on ending the Cold War in Europe to the global level.

CHAPTER 3

Operation Desert Shield and the Decision for War

Iraq's invasion of Kuwait was both a crisis and opportunity for Bush's New World Order grand strategy. By August 1990 the Bush administration was actively promoting political and economic liberalization in Central and Eastern Europe, working to incorporate a reunified Germany into a transformed NATO, and seeking to integrate a reforming Soviet Union into the Western political-economic order. While Bush's grand strategy had a global dimension, Washington was primarily concerned with European developments; US policies toward Asia, Latin America, and the Middle East were designed to insulate the positive trends in Europe from instability elsewhere in the world. In this context, Bush viewed Saddam Hussein's invasion of Kuwait as a destabilizing act of aggression that threatened the post–Cold War order he aspired to create. Saddam's actions tested the material, psychological, and normative underpinnings of American global leadership. Specifically, Iraq's invasion threatened to disrupt the flow of oil from the Persian Gulf and weaken the American economy at a critical time, challenged the credibility of American commitments to defend allies and partners against aggression, and endangered the prospects of an international system predicated on collective security and international law.

Much more than Kuwait's future was at stake in the Gulf crisis. The United States had to respond to Saddam's aggression, Bush believed, but the nature of its response would make or break the new world order. Seizing the moment, Bush attempted to elevate the main precepts of his grand strategy to the global level by adding two missing pieces to American statecraft: cooperation with the Soviet Union in resolving security challenges outside Europe and anchoring the new world order in the United Nations system.

Saddam's Invasion and Bush's Grand Strategy

Iraq's preparation for war was no secret. Beginning in mid-July 1990, the US government received a steady stream of intelligence pertaining to the Republican Guard's deployment to areas adjacent to the Iraq-Kuwait border.[1] In a speech on July 17 commemorating his country's national independence, Saddam lambasted "imperialists" and "Zionists" who sought to weaken Iraq's economy and exert control over the Middle East. Saddam charged that some Gulf states were colluding with the United States and Israel in this plot, "stabbing Iraq in the back with a poisoned dagger," and warned that "effective action" would be taken if the "bad behavior" continued. This was meant as an ultimatum, a point Iraq's foreign ministry underscored with its release of the text of Tariq Aziz's July 15 speech to the Arab League describing Kuwait's "theft" of Iraqi oil revenue as an act of "military aggression."[2]

These ominous signals were the subject of several meetings US ambassador to Iraq April Glaspie had with Iraqi officials, including a meeting with Saddam on July 26. After pressing the Iraqi president about his intentions, Glaspie told Saddam that while it had no "opinion on inter-Arab disputes like your border dispute with Kuwait," the United States "could never excuse settlement of disputes by any but peaceful means."[3] Glaspie was relieved to hear from Saddam that Egypt's president Hosni Mubarak had taken the lead in mediating the Iraq-Kuwait dispute. Mubarak, for his part, was confident that an Arab solution to the crisis could be found. Indeed, few of the region's leaders believed Iraq posed a genuine military threat to its neighbor. On July 31 King Hussein of Jordan reassured Bush that the issue would be resolved without the use of force. The Iraqis "have been through a war of eight years, a terrible experience for the country," the king told Bush. "They need to repair and for that, stable oil prices are necessary."[4] Bush left this conversation believing that a resolution to the immediate crisis was in the offing.[5]

The mismatch between the information Bush gleaned from diplomatic sources (including from the region's leaders) and intelligence he received regarding Iraq's military buildup could not have been starker. As a result, although few in the administration were surprised when Iraq's military rolled across the border, little attention had been devoted to the question of how the United States would respond to an invasion of Kuwait.[6] Upon learning of Saddam's decision, Scowcroft chaired what would be the first of fifty-five DC meetings covering the Gulf crisis and ensuing war.[7] The DC recommended that Saudi Arabia be offered a squadron of twenty-four F-15s, a signal of US commitment to the kingdom's territorial integrity, and that Iraq's financial assets be frozen immediately.[8] Additionally, at the urging of Secretary of State James Baker and Under Secretary of State Robert Kimmitt, the US ambassador to the United Nations Thomas Pickering orchestrated the passing of UN Security Council Resolution (UNSCR) 660, which condemned Iraq's invasion.[9]

The first NSC meeting on the unfolding crisis, held on August 2, proved disappointing to Bush and Scowcroft. Many of the participants seemed to take a dismissive view of the implications for American interests if Saddam's aggression went unanswered.[10] Discussions with Britain's prime minister Margaret Thatcher later that day in Aspen, Colorado were markedly different. It was at that meeting, Scowcroft admitted, that the significance of Saddam's action became apparent to Bush.[11] By the second NSC meeting on August 3, Bush's determination to confront Saddam had grown. To set the tone for the discussions, Scowcroft gave what NSC staffer Richard Haass called the "Churchill speech . . . a rousing call for the imperative of resisting and, in the end, reversing Iraqi aggression."[12] Whereas the national security adviser noted that an unchecked Saddam would be free to "dominate OPEC politics, Palestinian politics and the PLO, and lead the Arab world to the detriment of the United States," it was Deputy Secretary of State Lawrence Eagleburger who spelled out the larger grand strategic implications of Saddam's actions.

This is the first test of the post war system.[13] As the bipolar contest is relaxed, it permits this [aggression], giving people more flexibility because they are not worried about the involvement of the superpowers. The Soviets have come down hard. Saddam Hussein now has greater flexibility because the Soviets are tangled up in domestic issues. If he succeeds, others may try the same thing. It would be a bad lesson.

For Bush, all of this amounted to a status quo that was "intolerable."[14] Although the second NSC meeting concluded without a formal strategic decision, a clear direction was set. Scowcroft and Haass both stated that US policy should be to expel Iraqi forces from Kuwait but critically not to seek the overthrow of Saddam's regime. Furthermore, the United States would employ economic leverage against Iraq in the short term—an effort enhanced by the passage three days later of USCR 661, which slapped broad sanctions on Iraq. Finally, the meeting showed the president beginning to think about the use of force against Iraq, whose military, Chairman of the Joint Chiefs of Staff Colin Powell urged, should be taken seriously.

The third NSC meeting on August 4 focused on the military options available to the United States. General Norman Schwarzkopf, commander of US Central Command (CENTCOM), assessed it would take seventeen weeks to amass a military presence sufficient to blunt an Iraqi attack on Saudi Arabia—according to Powell a force consisting of roughly one hundred thousand troops.[15] A force of at least double that size would be needed to eject the Iraqi military from Kuwait. Should Bush decide on this offensive option, Schwarzkopf estimated that it would take a whopping eight to ten months to get the force ready to fight.[16] Even worse, there was virtually no way to stop Iraq from attacking Saudi Arabia in the short run. As Powell observed, the kingdom "is not doing much to prepare for any of this now," and Riyadh had yet to agree to host any American military assets on its territory. "We have a chicken and egg problem," Scowcroft summarized. The Saudis "don't want to get out in front and be left vulnerable, and we want to see if they have the will [to resist Saddam]."[17] After the meeting, Bush phoned King Fahd to inform him that Secretary of Defense Richard Cheney would meet with him to discuss plans for the defense of Saudi Arabia.[18] To underscore America's commitment to the kingdom's security, Bush told

Fahd, "The security of Saudi Arabia is vital—basically fundamental—to US interests and really to the interests of the western world. And I am determined that Saddam will not get away with this infamy."[19] The next day, Bush made this commitment public. To a group of reporters assembled outside the White House, Bush stated, "This will not stand, this aggression against Kuwait."[20]

By August 5 Bush, Scowcroft, Baker, and Cheney had concluded that Saddam's invasion of Kuwait had to be reversed. The three NSC meetings reveal a set of related strategic motives informing the administration's calculations. The first was the fear that Saddam's post-invasion position gave him an unacceptable level of influence over international oil markets. Not only had Iraq acquired new oil fields in Kuwait, but its military deployments near Saudi territory made the kingdom vulnerable to coercion—a situation the Bush administration deemed unacceptable to American interests due to the adverse effects it would have on the health of the global economy.[21] As Baker explained to the Senate Foreign Relations Committee in September, Saddam was "a dictator who, acting alone and unchallenged, could strangle the global economic order, determining by fiat, if you will, whether we all enter . . . [a] recession or whether even when we enter the darkness of a depression."[22] In addition to the administration's concern about the future of American prosperity, the prospect of an economic downturn threatened the United States' ability to conduct an active foreign policy at an inflection point in world history.[23]

Second, Saddam's aggression occurred at the very moment the Soviet Union was consumed by dramatic domestic and international events. Moscow's demonstrated inability to influence its supposed client meant that others, in the Middle East and elsewhere, could possibly use military force to achieve objectives the superpowers had previously denied. In such a permissive international environment, administration officials believed the United States had to reinforce the credibility of its security commitments to its allies and partners around the world. Exercising leadership and bolstering the credibility of US commitments meant not only challenging aggressive dictators (which British prime minister Neville Chamberlain failed to do in his meeting with Adolf Hitler at Munich in 1938) but also exorcising the ghosts of the Vietnam War, the belief held by many, including Saddam, that America lacked the fortitude to fight.²⁴ While the United States possessed overwhelming military might, that power would matter little to the future of general deterrence if a textbook case of aggression went unanswered. As Scowcroft argued in a memo to Bush early in the crisis, a failure to act decisively would set "a terrible precedent—one that would only accelerate violent centrifugal tendencies—in this emerging 'post-Cold War' era."²⁵

It was the challenge to the emerging world order, however, that most profoundly motivated officials in the White House and State Department to confront Saddam and determined how that confrontation occurred. In addition to the strength of the American economy and the credibility of its security commitments to its allies and partners, the administration saw two additional factors at stake in the crisis: the dramatically improved relationship that Washington and Moscow had forged over the past year and a half, and international norms—sovereignty, territorial integrity, and respect for international law—that served as the foundation for peace and stability in the order Bush desired to create.

As already suggested, Saddam's invasion of Kuwait offered Bush the opportunity to achieve a central objective of his New World Order grand strategy, the integration of the Soviet Union into the Western international order. As stipulated in NSD-23, the secretary of state was tasked to look for opportunities to partner with the Soviets to resolve threats to the stability of regions around the world. Consistent with that strategic vision, Baker launched an intensive diplomatic campaign to secure not merely Moscow's acceptance of American policy but active Soviet assistance in employing it. The day after Iraq's invasion, Baker met with Shevardnadze in Moscow. At the outset of that meeting Baker stated,

> I've come here because I thought it important to demonstrate that we can and will act as partners in facing new challenges to international security. While it is easy to talk about partnership, taking the unusual step of issuing a joint call for an international cutoff of arms would send a signal to the world and to the Iraqis that U.S.-Soviet partnership is real. It would also send a signal that together we have entered a new era and would demonstrate that when a crisis de-

velops, we're prepared to act swiftly and affirmatively in a meaningful way.

Shevardnadze agreed, telling the press afterwards that Saddam's "aggression is inconsistent with the principles of new thinking and, in fact, with the civilized relations between nations."[26]

Soviet support would be critical to the forging of an international coalition to reverse Iraq's invasion. While he had successfully elicited Moscow's support in condemning the aggression, Baker hoped for more from the Soviet Union. Operation Desert Shield, which consisted of a buildup of military forces in Saudi Arabia to deter further Iraqi aggression, commenced on August 6, after Cheney's successful visit to Riyadh.[27] The next day, Baker phoned Shevardnadze to let him know that US troops would be heading to the Gulf. The Soviet foreign minister was displeased to hear that Bush had approved military action; Shevardnadze charged that Baker's call wasn't to "consult" but rather to inform him of an action already taken. "The Soviet Union would consider this action exceptional, extraordinary and temporary," Shevardnadze told Baker, adding that American "military force should leave as quickly as possible." Baker reassured Shevardnadze that "no offensive actions were planned" and that the deployment, "taken at the request of the Saudis," was "strictly to deter."[28] Baker then pivoted, stating, "I would like to explore with you whether Soviet forces would want to participate with the U.S. in a multinational force. This would demonstrate resolve and make the use of force less likely." The next day, Shevardnadze informed Baker that the Soviets would not contribute forces to Desert Shield. Nonetheless, Baker believed Moscow's sensibilities regarding the US deployment of military forces to the region had been assuaged.[29]

While pleased with Baker's progress, Bush wanted to send a clearer message to Saddam and the world that the United States and Soviet Union were united in their opposition to Iraq's aggression. In a quickly convened meeting in Helsinki on September 9, Bush stressed to Gorbachev that if international sanctions failed, the coalition would have to forcibly remove the Iraqi military from Kuwait. "I needed to convince him," Bush recalled, "that the best way to create a new world order of

Soviet-American cooperation against aggression was to support a strong response, which would have implications for the future of world peace." Bush emphasized that the crisis presented the two countries with an opportunity: "The closer we come today, the closer the new world order.... I want to work with you as equal partners in dealing with this." Bush then reiterated the offer that Baker had made to Shevardnadze, that Soviet forces would be welcomed in the international military coalition, an exchange that left the more cautious Scowcroft uneasy. Allaying the national security adviser's concerns, Gorbachev did not respond to Bush, and the matter was dropped. Gorbachev did respond positively to Bush's vision, however, concurring with the president that resolving the crisis was a prerequisite for the new world order.[30] Anatoly Chernyaev, Gorbachev's top foreign policy adviser, later explained that Bush and Gorbachev "shared the same broad goals—to settle the Gulf conflict, and in so doing reinforce the new Soviet-American relations and advance the new world order," an international system based on "international law and the principles of the U.N."[31]

Yet, to Gorbachev's way of thinking, the new world order should not be predicated on the use of force. The Soviet leader proposed instead an international conference to deal comprehensively with Middle East regional security issues, including the Israeli-Palestinian conflict. Fearing that such a plan would enable Saddam's ambitions, Bush rejected the idea of holding a conference before the Gulf crisis had been resolved. In the abstract, however, the president was open to the idea, and the two sides privately agreed that once the Gulf crisis was resolved satisfactorily, "we would work with countries inside and outside the region to develop security structures and measures to promote peace and stability." Overall, the Helsinki meeting was a success for Bush. The joint communique stated, "We are determined to see this crisis to the end, and if current steps fail to end it, we are prepared to consider additional ones consistent with the UN charter. We must demonstrate beyond any doubt that aggression cannot and will not pay."[32]

American objectives in the Gulf crisis were specified in NSD-45 on August 20: the complete and unconditional withdrawal of Iraqi forces from Kuwait, the restoration of the Kuwaiti government, a commitment to regional security and stability, and the safety of Americans abroad.[33]

On September 11, in a speech to a joint session of Congress, Bush added a fifth objective, leveraging the crisis to bring into being a new world order, a world "freer from the threat of terror, stronger in the pursuit of justice, and more secure in the quest for peace.... A world where the rule of law supplants the rule of the jungle. A world in which nations recognize the shared responsibility for freedom and justice. A world where the strong respect the rights of the weak." In conjunction with the president's speeches in Hamtramck and Mainz on democracy in Central-East Europe and German unification, the NATO summit communique that cleared the way for German accession to NATO, and NSD-23 (which laid out the goal of integrating the Soviet Union into the Western community of nations), Bush's speech on the Gulf crisis served as the culmination of the administration's New World Order grand strategy.

Bush's goal was to elevate Washington's strategic approach toward Europe to the global level, to argue that an historic opportunity was at hand to make the world freer and safer. Critical to this effort was extensive great power cooperation and, through the UN, multilateral solutions to complex security problems. "I am pleased that we [the United States and USSR] are working together to build a new relationship," Bush declared. "In Helsinki, our joint statement affirmed to the world our shared resolve to counter Iraq's threat to peace.... Clearly, no longer can a dictator count on East-West confrontation to stymie concerted United Nations action against aggression. A new partnership has begun." Informing his audience that his vision for a new era of international partnership was possible in the aftermath of the Cold War, Bush stated that Saddam's challenge required the cooperation of all nations. Gorbachev "and other leaders from Europe, the Gulf, and around the world understand that how we manage this crisis today could shape the future for generations to come." Bush insisted that the United States would, working with other states, act in support of "the new world that we seek," defend "common vital interests," and "stand up to aggression." American leadership was critical to the forging of a broad international coalition to confront Saddam. And the UN would play a central role in the new world order. "We're now in sight of a United Nations that performs as envisioned by its founders.... The United Nations is backing up its words with action."[34] By reviving the mechanism of collective security, not only would the world benefit but so too would the United States.

Bush's post–Cold War vision was not one of American primacy cloaked in the rhetoric of international cooperation. Elaborating on the logic of his strategic approach, Bush highlighted the role that Soviet-American cooperation played in allowing the UN "Security Council to operate as its founders had envisioned," a necessary condition in the new world order. "Our foundation was the premise that the United States henceforth would be obligated to lead the world community to an unprecedented degree," Bush recalled, "and we should attempt to pursue our national interests, wherever possible within a framework of concert with our friends and the international community."[35] Working in concert with other states meant accepting restrictions on US policy autonomy. While recognizing that there would be a role for the United States in the Gulf after the war, Bush made clear in his speech to Congress that American policy would be limited to facilitating deterrence and "to help[ing] our friends in their own self-defense."

While US military power served as the vital foundation of American leadership, the logic of Bush's strategy implied that the United States would be both more secure *and* able to reduce the size of the American military and defense budgets. The economic component to Bush's speech, a section that often goes unmentioned in the literature, offers an important lens for viewing the president's strategic objectives. "Congress should, this month, enact a prudent multiyear defense program," Bush declared, "one that reflects not only the improvement in East-West relations but our broader responsibilities to deal with the continuing risks of outlaw action and regional conflict. Even with our obligations in the Gulf, a sound defense budget can have some reduction in real terms; and we're prepared to accept that." Moreover, while international burden-sharing offered a means by which countries around the world could support the new world order, it was also a way of alleviating the financial burden of war. "The material cost of leadership can be steep," Bush argued. "The burden of this collective effort must be shared. We are prepared to do our share and more to help carry that load; we insist that others do their share as well."[36] In sum, Bush envisioned a world order based on collective action. Not only would security and prosperity be enhanced through great power cooperation but the order would also be sustainable in the long run.

Elaborating further on his grand strategic objectives in a speech in Prague in November, Bush invoked the concept of a "commonwealth for freedom" wherein the rule of law governed the affairs of nations. Open to all states, this commonwealth would be "a moral community united in its dedication to free ideals." Binding together the various elements of his strategic approach, Bush asserted that the "great and growing strength of the commonwealth of freedom [would] forge for all nations a new world order far more stable and secure than any we have ever known."[37] Encapsulating the logic of Bush's grand strategy, Henry Kissinger summarized, "A peaceful world would now unfold, so long as the democracies took care to assist the final wave of democratic transformations in countries still under authoritarian rule. The ultimate Wilsonian vision would be fulfilled. Free political and economic institutions would spread and eventually submerge outdated antagonisms in a broader harmony."[38]

The New World Order grand strategy was indeed Wilsonian, a distinctly American style of liberal internationalism.[39] Bush's strategic approach explicitly tied American security to global peace and stability. As Tony Smith explains, Wilsonianism contains four pillars: democracy promotion, collective security, free trade, and American leadership in the international system. All of these were elements of Bush's grand strategy.[40] Washington's foreign policy from spring 1989 to September 1990 had been focused on encouraging democracy in Central and Eastern Europe and incorporating a liberalizing Soviet Union in the Western international political economic order. Saddam Hussein's invasion of Kuwait afforded Bush the opportunity to exercise American leadership to revive the moribund collective security function at the heart of the UN system.

Coercive Diplomacy and Coalition Building

The United States implemented a comprehensive coercive diplomacy campaign against Iraq, the outlines of which were neatly summarized by Baker:

> We would begin with diplomatic pressure, then add economic pressure, to a great degree organized through the United Nations, and finally move toward military pressure by gradually increasing American troop strength in the Gulf. The strategy was to lead a global political alliance aimed at isolating Iraq. Through the use of economic sanctions, we hoped to make Saddam pay such a high price for his aggression that in time he would be forced to release his Western hostages and withdraw from Kuwait. If he didn't, we would expel him by military force.[41]

The "global political alliance" Baker referenced comprised three overlapping coalitions: political, military, and financial. "The membership and roles in these three coalitions overlap, but are not identical, and all had their own problems," Philip Zelikow recalled. It was "a fantastically intricate piece of work—for which it's very difficult to find any precedent short of going back to Britain in the Napoleonic Wars."[42] Aligning these coalitions to serve a common purpose fell to Scowcroft and the NSC staff—though Scowcroft maintains the lion's share of the credit went to Bush. "I think the key to all of these coalitions was the President and his performance in handholding, cajoling, leading, urging the members of the various coalitions to keep them all together."[43]

The financial coalition was important in two respects. First, Saddam's invasion of Kuwait occurred as the administration was attempting to reach a budget compromise with Congress. After years of budget deficits caused by Reagan-era defense spending and tax cuts, the Bush administration faced significant fiscal constraints. It was thus important to Bush that coalition members provide not simply token military support to the US effort in the Gulf but rather significant financial contributions. To that end, Baker embarked on an eleven-day trip to nine states to elicit financial support—an effort dubbed "tin cup diplomacy." The results were impressive, with Saudi Arabia and the Emir of Kuwait each providing upward of $16 billion on the spot. All told, the United States received $54.5 billion to cover the cost associated with the crisis and war; the United Kingdom received an addition £2 billion.[44] Second, the financial coalition helped Washington keep a critical member of the political coalition on board. While attending a 2+4 ministerial meeting in Moscow on September 12, Gorbachev asked Baker to ask if Saudi Arabia would provide $4–5 billion to assist the embattled Soviet economy.[45] The Saudis agreed to a $4 billion line of credit, which, in Baker's estimation, was "instrumental in solidifying Soviet support for the use-of-force resolution and keeping them firmly in the coalition throughout the crisis."[46]

The United Nations was central to Bush's grand strategy, specifically due to the organization's collective security function. As we have seen, Bush valued the UN as a forum where American political leadership could be exercised to help find common ground among countries. There were elements of both normative principle and tactical efficiency to Bush's views regarding the UN. The president valued the organization's commitment to the sanctity of national sovereignty and viewed agreements among sovereign states under the UN's umbrella as being particularly meaningful, an expression of the will of the international community. At the same time, Bush understood that America's preferred policies would face weakened resistance if they were crafted through the UN. As Haass summarized, the administration knew that "for most people around the world and their governments the U.N. is an important and at times essential source of authority and legitimacy. Its endorsement can constitute a prerequisite for the participation of others, be it to make sanctions effective or lend support to U.S. military efforts or to introduce forces of their own."[47] Forging agreements with other governments often requires assuaging foreign publics, a role that the UN is uniquely capable of fulfilling.[48]

Sustaining an international consensus against Iraqi aggression was no easy task. Saddam was seen by many in the Middle East as the embodiment of Arab nationalism, and the prospect of US forces stationed in the region on a semipermanent basis smacked of neocolonialism.[49] Additionally, the use of force against Iraq threatened countries with close economic ties to Baghdad, most notably Egypt, Turkey, and Syria.[50] Similarly, many in governments outside the Middle East were skeptical—if not outright hostile—to the deployment and possible use of US military forces in the region. Many Soviet officials objected to Gorbachev's support of American security policy, especially those in the military and foreign ministry.[51] France was the Western country with the most extensive economic ties to Iraq, and many there objected to signing on to an American-sponsored war that could cost the French economy dearly.[52]

Yet, a durable international consensus against Iraq was critical to Bush's grand strategic commitment to collective security in the new world order. It fell to America's ambassador to the United Nations Thomas Pickering to spearhead the political coalition-building effort. Pickering approached the challenge in three ways. The first was to create a sense of urgency in the Security Council by stringing together a series of resolutions that together laid the legal ground for a truly multilateral effort to expel Iraq from Kuwait. Yet because the UN's collective security mechanism was moribund after years of Cold War political division, Pickering found that he had to convince Security Council members that the body could, in fact, handle this core responsibility embodied in the UN's charter. "The way to do that," Pickering later described, was "to make [the Security Council] feel, for the moment at least, it is the most important club in the world." The constant glare of the international media aided in this respect, as did Saddam Hussein. "We didn't have to confect a lot of things to go to next because Saddam was the perfect opponent," Pickering noted. "He gave us problems that led to resolutions."[53]

Second, to prevent Saddam from weaseling out from under UN-imposed obligations, Pickering ensured that all the resolutions related to the crisis were cast under chapter VII of the UN charter—specifically, the provision binding all member states to decisions agreed upon by the Security Council. "This was very unusual," Pickering explained, "because up until then ... the Council rarely used the mandatory provisions." Leveraging chapter VII was a consequential choice because it prevented UN member states from negotiating with Saddam "outside the four walls of those resolutions" to reach a compromise settlement to the crisis.[54] As historian Paul Kennedy noted, Saddam again aided the American effort by offering "the classic case for the Security Council to authorize military action under Chapter VII ... a perfect example of what the planners of 1944-45 contemplated."[55]

To both minimize the chance that third parties would seek a negotiated settlement outside UN resolutions and to illustrate the extent to which Saddam had turned Iraq into an international pariah, Pickering's third tactic was to get as many UN Security Council members as possible to vote in favor of the resolutions. The most important target of this effort was China, a permanent member endowed with veto power. Pickering's problem was that China took a principled stance against the Security Council authorizing the use of military force against a UN member state. To get around this obstacle, Pickering worked with the Chinese ambassador to the UN to allow Beijing to register its objections to such authorizations, but without exercising its veto. This included crafting language in the resolutions that enabled the Chinese to abstain from voting on critical resolutions, including UNSCR 678, which authorized states to "use all necessary means" against Iraq if it failed to withdraw from Kuwait on or before January 15, 1991.[56] China's willingness to abstain from, rather than veto, UNSCR 678 was also aided by Bush's strategic decision to maintain ties with Beijing following the Tiananmen massacre, a move that drew considerable congressional fire. "China remembered the terrible savaging Bush took for them," US ambassador to China James Lilley recalled. "And when it came time to collect the fee for that, he could do it."[57]

Ultimately, Bush didn't need to work through the United Nations. But he understood that a new world order, grounded in international law and respect for national sovereignty, demanded a degree of global multilateralism not seen since the end of World War II. Bush also knew that forging a collective response to Iraqi aggression meant that he would have to accept limits on America's own behavior. It thus mattered greatly that US objectives and actions were tied to the twelve UN Security Council resolutions passed between August 2 and November 29. At critical points before the war, Bush showed that he respected the will of the international community by delaying action until the Security Council had fully weighed in. Passed on August 6, UNSCR 661, for example, imposed tight economic sanctions and embargoed arms shipments to Iraq. That resolution did not, however, contain explicit language regarding how military force would be used to enforce the embargo. Almost immediately, Bush was confronted with calls to interdict ships destined for Iraqi ports. The US military wanted to begin interdiction operations right away and, if necessary, unilaterally. Upon learning of the military's willingness to go it alone, Pickering informed Baker that failing to secure a resolution explicitly granting the use of force to impose the embargo would mean walking "away from the Security Council ... [and] away from all the support this huge anchor that we have built gives us, the whole juridical business that gave ... a strong basis in legitimacy internationally in what we were doing."[58] Bush was persuaded, ordering US naval forces to impose the embargo only on August 31—six days after the passage of UNSCR 665 authorizing the halting of all inbound and outbound ships to Iraq.

By showing his commitment to the letter of the law and to working through the UN, Bush was able to build a diverse political coalition that effectively isolated Iraq from the international community. Chief among the factors binding the political coalition together was America's willingness to self-impose restrictions on its freedom of maneuver and limitations to its objectives.[59] In other words, it wasn't only the widely held belief that Saddam Hussein was in the wrong and needed to be punished that kept coalition members on board. Just as important was the sense that coalition members could influence the United States and that their actions made a difference to global peace and security. "In the name of establishing a new criteria of world politics, old means had to be used—military force," Gorbachev's adviser Anatoly Chernyaev wrote in his memoir. "But if Gorbachev hadn't been one of the key actors, the use of those means would have gone beyond the U.N. framework. And this would have jeopardized much of what had recently been accomplished to improve international relations."[60] Bush, Baker, and Pickering all understood that collective security required not just a shared sense of purpose among states but, just as critically, a belief that each state's political contribution was valuable in some important way.

The same sense of collective mission infused the military coalition. Critical to the coalition's effectiveness (indeed, its existence) was the active participation by states in the region. As mentioned, Egyptian president Hosni Mubarak had hoped that a resolution to the Iraq-Kuwait dispute could be brokered short of war. Saddam's decision to invade rendered an Arab solution all but impossible to reach. The attempt to keep the crisis "in the family" was undermined by three factors. First, the UN Security Council's prompt condemnation of Iraqi aggression effectively globalized the regional dispute, a move that stripped away the ability of states neighboring Iraq to set the agenda. Second, the decision by Riyadh to accept the American offer to station its military forces in the kingdom magnified Saudi Arabia's security dependence on the United States. Finally, opinion among Arab states over the best course of action was sharply divided, but the three most consequential countries—Saudi Arabia, Egypt, and Syria—all demanded a complete withdrawal of Iraqi forces from Kuwait.[61]

The military coalition that constituted Desert Shield—and eventually Desert Storm—included both frontline states and countries further afield. Although the United States was by far the most powerful nation in the coalition and the largest contributor of troops and materiel, the extent of burden sharing among coalition members attenuated the power disparity somewhat. The largest military coalition to form since World War II, Desert Shield assembled countries with diverse (and potentially divisive) political and cultural backgrounds. Recognizing the challenge, the US military took steps to enhance the cohesion of the coalition. For example, US troops deployed to Saudi Arabia received extensive briefings on the region's history, customs, religions, and laws. Further, as Patricia Weitsman explains,

> Alcohol was prohibited in the CENTCOM area of operation, and a civilian dress code was established as well. Broadcasts on the U.S. Armed Forces radio and television services were monitored to avoid offense. American women were briefed extensively regarding Islamic and Saudi expectations of female conduct, although the Saudis did lift the prohibition against women driving, providing that it was part of their official duty.

For his part, CENTCOM commander Norman Schwarzkopf went to great lengths to accommodate nations with distinctive perspectives, acting as much as a diplomat as a military commander—notwithstanding the general's legendary temper. Finally, as a result of the high degree of cohesion exhibited in the first months of the crisis, the coalition itself became a source of legitimacy for the coercive campaign against Iraq.[62]

The Decision for War

Operation Desert Shield had two objectives: to deter an Iraqi attack on Saudi Arabia and to provide the military component of the coercion campaign against Saddam. Pressure began mounting as early as mid-August to abandon coercive diplomacy in favor of an offensive military response. On August 16 Saudi foreign minister Saud al-Faisal met with Bush and his senior advisers in Kennebunkport, Maine. Speaking on behalf of Riyadh, Cairo, and Damascus, Prince Saud stated, "Our assessment is that it will take more than economic sanctions to liberate Kuwait." Saud urged Bush to take whatever steps were necessary to not merely liberate Kuwait but also to destroy as much of Saddam's war-making capacity as possible. Saud's message showed the extent to which these three frontline states perceived Saddam to be an acute and long-term threat.[63]

By mid-September, CENTCOM intelligence revealed that the coalition's deterrence effort was succeeding. Iraqi tank units had been moved away from the Iraq's border with Saudi Arabia and replaced by tens of thousands of entrenched infantry units preparing for a lengthy siege. At the same time, Saddam showed no intention of withdrawing from Kuwait. In fact, the opposite appeared to be the case. "Troops were still pouring into Kuwait and the neighboring parts of Iraq," Schwarzkopf recalled. "When I'd briefed President Bush at Camp David [on August 4], we'd talked about an Iraqi force of 100,000 soldiers and 850 tanks in Kuwait, but we soon found ourselves facing more than *one third of a million soldiers* and 2,750 tanks. The Iraqis had also wheeled in nearly 1,500 artillery pieces capable, we knew, of firing toxic-chemical shells."[64]

Despite Saddam's military reinforcements in Kuwait and southeastern Iraq, UN-imposed economic sanctions by that time had cut off almost 95 percent of Iraq's exports and imports; moreover, Saddam was almost completely isolated diplomatically. The apparent effectiveness of these nonmilitary measures convinced Powell that a war to liberate Kuwait was unnecessary. "Containment" (more accurately, strangulation), the chairman of the joint chiefs of staff believed, was the appropriate policy for getting Iraq out of Kuwait. Powell pitched this idea to Undersecretary of Defense Paul Wolfowitz, stating that he believed Saddam would likely come to terms in a month's time. Unconvinced, Wolfowitz countered that Saddam had to believe that sanctions would be in place indefinitely if they were to stand any chance of working. Still, Powell made his case separately to Cheney and Scowcroft, as well as to Baker—the senior official most in favor of a diplomatic solution to the crisis. Finally, on September 24 Powell met with Bush, Scowcroft, and Cheney in the Oval Office. The chairman of the Joint Chiefs told Bush that Iraq could be dislodged from Kuwait either through war or containment. Both would work, Powell estimated, but containment would require less of a military investment and court fewer risks. To achieve maximum effect, the containment option needed a force of about 230,000 troops, the level that would be reached by December 1. "Saddam would be fully boxed in," Powell assured Bush. "Containment would grind him down." But Bush wasn't convinced, stating, "I don't think there's time politically for that strategy." To Powell, this response indicated that while Bush was a containment skeptic, he had not yet fully committed to either course of action.[65] In any case, the president had not yet issued the explicit order that the US military required to either continue or throttle back the flow of forces to the theater.[66]

Bush's determination for war was stiffened by his meeting with the emir of Kuwait, Jaber al-Ahmad al-Sabah, on September 28. Jaber gave Bush a detailed account of the atrocities Iraqi forces were committing in his country. "It was during this period," Bush recounted, "that I began to move from viewing Saddam's aggression exclusively as a dangerous strategic threat and an injustice to its reversal as a moral crusade."[67] In Bush's mind, and increasingly in his public statements, the parallels between Saddam Hussein and Adolf Hitler were strong. "What is at stake is whether the nations of the world can take a common stand against aggression," Bush declared in Dallas on October 15, insisting that Saddam's actions were tantamount to "Hitler revisited." Bush's comparisons to Hitler in particular worried Powell, who "thought it unwise to elevate public expectations by making the man out to be the devil incarnate and then leave him in place," the most likely outcome of a war fought to liberate Kuwait.[68]

The Deputies Committee met in early October to debate whether and how the coercion campaign should transition to a mission of liberation.

DC members neither had confidence that sanctions would prove effective nor believed that the United States should wait for Saddam to offer some additional justification before commencing an attack. Rather, the DC concluded that a UN-backed ultimatum should be issued, demanding Iraq exit Kuwait by a certain date.[69] In late October US ambassador to Saudi Arabia Chas Freeman cabled Baker and Bush with news that officials in Riyadh were beginning to insist that the crisis be resolved quickly—if necessary, by war. In contrast to Baker, Freeman argued that time was not on America's side, because Saddam would have more opportunities to splinter the coalition the longer Washington delayed. Given that Ramadan would begin on March 18, Freeman counseled that all military operations needed to be completed by the first week of March 1991. As such, "judgments had to be made NOW on whether we need to have an offensive option in order to resolve this crisis, because the favorable window for utilizing such an option begins to close just three months from now, by end of January."[70]

Bush's core group of advisers met in the Situation Room to discuss both Freeman's memo and the DC's recommendations. Although desiring a diplomatic solution to the crisis, Baker concluded that sanctions were unlikely to work in the timeframe Freeman suggested. Cheney then noted that a real offensive option would require the deployment of a substantial number of additional forces. Cheney was more inclined to use force to eject Iraq from Kuwait, but many uniformed military officers were not. As deputy national security adviser Robert Gates recalled, the "truth of the matter is that the military, the chiefs were very content with the deployment of 200,000 to 215,000 troops to Saudi Arabia that essentially protected Saudi Arabia, and they had no enthusiasm for an offensive effort to throw Saddam out." Powell did not dispute Gates's characterization of the chiefs' position. Reflecting on his own reputation for being a "reluctant warrior," Powell admitted, "Guilty. War is a deadly game; and I do not believe in spending the lives of Americans lightly. My responsibility that day was to lay out all the options for the nation's civilian leadership."[71]

Powell may have been a reluctant warrior, but he was not opposed to the use of force if the effort was resourced properly—that is, overwhelmingly. By this time, Schwarzkopf had already made the case that an additional army corps was needed to make any offensive ground attack option effective. Meeting with the CENTCOM commander in Riyadh on October 22, Powell said he agreed with Schwarzkopf's request and that he would also support sending an additional division from the United States. But that was not all.

> We would also send another Marine division. I beefed up his request for additional fighter squadrons. Aircraft carriers? Let's send six. We had paid for this stuff. Why not use it? What were we saving it for? We had learned a lesson in Panama. Go in big, and end it quickly. We could not put the United States through another Vietnam. We could be so lavish with resources because the world had changed. We could now afford to pull divisions out of Germany that had been there for the past forty years to stop a Soviet offensive that was no longer coming.[72]

Gates had extensive experience assisting presidents and their senior advisers make consequential national decisions, including whether to employ military force. That experience told him to be wary of military commanders' estimates of force level requirements. Since Vietnam, Gates maintained, the military had come to mistrust the willingness of civilian officials to use force. "Any time a President demands a contingency plan to consider, the military puts together a force that is so overwhelming that the President will balk at the cost and at the disruption and everything else and not do it." With all of this in mind, Gates sets the stage in an interview he gave in 2000:

> So the [military] briefer starts out, "First we'll need the Seventh Corps out of Germany." Okay, you're going to take the heart of NATO's defense ... [and] move it from Germany to Saudi Arabia, the two heaviest divisions in the American Army. Okay. "Then we'll need six carrier battle groups." We had never put six carrier battle groups in the same theater of action since there were aircraft carriers, and we're looking, that's sort of a hundred ships or something like that by the time you count all of the other stuff. ... Oh, and you'll have to activate both the National Guard and the Reserves." In other words,

you're going to reach into every community in America and take people away from their homes and their jobs.

But Bush didn't blink. Gates concludes,

> To the day I die I'll never forget, Bush pushed his chair back, stood up, looked at Cheney and said, "You've got it, let me know if you need more," and walked out of the room. Cheney's jaw dropped. Powell's jaw dropped. Cheney looks at Scowcroft and says, "Does he know what he just authorized?" And Brent smiled and he said, "He knows perfectly well what he authorized."[73]

Bush's decision on October 30 to more than double the force deployment to the theater (from roughly 215,000 to 540,000) made possible an offensive option to expel Iraq from Kuwait that senior military officers were comfortable with. But the decision to go to war had not yet been made. At that point, no UN Security Council resolution authorizing such a mission had been passed. It was to that end that Bush and Baker now devoted all their efforts.

Getting a resolution for war would require deft diplomacy, especially because three of the Security Council's five permanent member states were either opposed to, or wary about, the use of force. Up to this moment, China had been able to register its dissent on several resolutions without derailing the organization's efforts. But things were different now: Beijing recoiled at the idea that the United States could assume a hegemonic position in the Gulf through military means, accruing vast influence over that region's oil reserves. Further, Beijing calculated that China could reap reputational benefits by playing an instrumental role in preventing a major regional war, thereby regaining much of its international standing lost after Tiananmen. Meeting with China's foreign minister Qian Qichen in a Cairo airport lounge, Baker pointedly stated, "We don't hold it against our friends that they are not joining us.... But we *do* ask that they do not stand in the way." Qian didn't respond to Baker's blunt message, but the secretary of state believed it got through.[74]

At the end of October, Gorbachev met with French president Francois Mitterrand in Rambouillet to discuss the three-month-old crisis. The two found themselves in accord on most of the important issues.

Both were steadfast in their commitment to uphold the extant Security Council resolutions pertaining to Iraq's invasion of Kuwait. Yet, Gorbachev and Mitterrand also agreed that the use of force to enforce those resolutions would be a disaster, so much so that they were willing to entertain notions that the United States and Britain refused to consider. Gorbachev noted that Soviet diplomat Yevgeny Primakov—who had just met with Saddam—detected a softening in the Iraqi leader's stance, a possible willingness to look for a way out of the situation he had created. With this analysis as their starting point, Gorbachev and Mitterrand discussed possible methods of enticing Saddam to the negotiating table. They agreed that Saddam would now find an Arab solution to the crisis most appealing. Mitterrand went so far as to suggest that it wasn't "expedient to speak in favor of restoration of the Kuwaiti ruling dynasty" and that other concessions should be offered to Saddam, including "access to the Persian Gulf, oil prospecting, and others." For war to be avoided, Saddam had to have hope that he would be rewarded for conceding on the issue of Kuwaiti territory. At the very least, "Hussein's vanity would be assuaged," a critical step on the path toward a compromise solution. Gorbachev agreed, adding, "If we don't give Hussein anything, he will go to extremes."

But there was a problem, one that required Saddam to show his willingness to abandon territory very soon. Mitterrand pointed out that some in the United States believed that article 51 of the UN Charter (i.e., the self-defense provision) was sufficient legal justification for the use of force. The French president noted ominously that America could rationalize war if Saudi Arabia simply requested its assistance to resolve an immediate threat to the kingdom's territorial integrity. "It turns out that the United States, on their own, without recourse to the U.N. Security Council, could decide to start the war," Mitterrand warned. "If one could put it this way, they become the 'masters of war'."[75]

On November 8, Baker traveled to Moscow to persuade Gorbachev and Shevardnadze to support the idea of a new Security Council resolution authorizing the use of force. Baker began by expressing his satisfaction that the Saudis had come through on a sizable line of credit to help stabilize the Soviet economy, adding, "We were very happy we were able to help you out that way." Baker then assured Gorbachev that he and Bush hoped for a "peaceful, political resolution to the crisis." But, Baker insisted, "the madman with whom we have to deal will only leave Kuwait if he is convinced that we are serious and decisive." Time wasn't on their side, Baker argued, because Saddam was trying to split the coalition by playing to antiwar sentiments in the United States and elsewhere. The coalition's only recourse was to work together to adopt a Security Council resolution that would "sanction the use of all means necessary for ensuring implementation of all UN resolutions." Action needed to be taken now, Baker continued, because the chairmanship of the Security Council would pass from the United States to Iraq's ally Yemen in three weeks' time. Moreover, the threat of force had to be leveled early in the new year to avoid the onset of the rainy season, Ramadan, and the Hajj. The window of opportunity for concerted action was closing, and delay would threaten the readiness of the military forces amassed in Saudi Arabia.

America was determined to cooperate with the Soviet Union, Baker assured his hosts, adding, "I cannot stop thinking that if the use of force becomes necessary, the image of Americans and Russians fighting side by side (even if your participation is limited to a small unit) would made [*sic*] a very strong impression." Baker conceded that Saddam should be given more time—an additional two months—to comply with the UN's demands. "It is clear that we are not proposing any kind of premature or reckless action." Still, Saddam had to be confronted with the stark reality "that if he does not withdraw, force will be used." Embedded in Baker's remarks was a stark choice for Gorbachev, too. Baker admitted that there were some in the United States urging Bush to attack Iraq "on the basis of Article 51 of the UN Charter," rather than seek another Security Council resolution. "We very much want to act in accord with the entire international community. But I would like to inform you that the President is willing to assume responsibility for the dirtiest part of this operation because we are convinced that here we are talking about an important principle."[76] While Bush may not have wanted to be the "master of war," he was willing to act even if the Soviets weren't.[77]

Baker worked every conceivable angle in his "long and rather remarkable discussions" with Gorbachev and Shevardnadze. To his satisfaction, the secretary of state discovered the Soviets operating under two favorable assumptions: (1) that the fate of the US effort at the UN directly affected the prospects of the new world order and of perestroika, (2) that Saddam "must clearly unmistakably fail" in his annexation of Kuwait. At the same time, they felt that sanctions should be given more time to work before an ultimatum on the use of force was issued. Baker sensed that Gorbachev was persuaded by his logic that sanctions could only be effective if an even greater danger loomed in the future.[78] And indeed, Gorbachev agreed to support a use of force resolution on November 19 in a meeting with Bush in Paris. Gorbachev was ultimately persuaded by the US president's dedication to the principles of collective security, realizing that Bush was taking the "right and responsible position" by not acting based on article 51 authority. Only by concerted action through the UN, Gorbachev insisted, could the Soviet Union and the United States create a world freer from the threats of "aggression, annexation, and blanket violation of international law."[79] With the stakes so high, Gorbachev concluded he could not afford to abandon the United States at the UN.

The meeting of the Security Council on November 29 was convened at the ministerial level, a signal to the world that the topic of the day's proceedings was of the gravest importance. As the council's chairman, Baker kicked off the meeting stating, "With the Cold War behind us, we now have the chance to build a world which was envisioned by this organization, by the founders of the United Nations." Resolution 678 passed 12–2 with one abstention. Predictably, Cuba and Yemen were the dissenting votes, while China registered its objection without vetoing the measure. While the resolution included the phrase "all necessary means," Baker made clear that the use of force should be authorized if Saddam did not completely withdraw his forces from Kuwait. Iraq was given until January 15, 1991, to demonstrate its full compliance.[80]

George Bush had been moving toward this moment since early August. Now, with the passage of UNSCR 678, the Security Council demonstrated that it could function as the collective security institution envisioned in the UN Charter.[81] Saddam Hussein's persistent refusal to abide by the will of the international community to restore the status quo ante created the conditions for Bush to work cooperatively with the Soviet Union to resolve security challenges outside Europe and to establish the UN's collective security mechanism as the cornerstone of the new world order. The question now was whether Saddam would comply or face the consequences.

Many in the administration, including Bush, now saw war as the preferred outcome of the crisis. After receiving a detailed briefing from Schwarzkopf on Thanksgiving Day, Bush believed that the US military would make short work of Saddam's forces.[82] Given the coalition forces' size and capabilities, the anticipated costs of war were acceptable. Avoiding armed conflict, moreover, courted substantial risk. Senior NSC officials worried that Saddam could make a "tactical move that would pre-empt an attack; that would allow him to loot the country, and not get punished, and remain a major menace." Among all conceivable outcomes, Gates concluded, war was "absolutely preferrable." The possibility of Saddam's military force remaining intact after a partial withdrawal was disconcerting because the massive but idle force deployed by the international coalition simply wasn't sustainable for much longer. Haass feared that if the United States opted not to go to war, Saddam would retain the capacity to threaten Kuwait and Saudi Arabia, while at the same time undercutting any justification for a future coalition attack should it prove necessary. A war aimed at liberating Kuwait and degrading Iraq's military capacity would obviate all these problems.[83]

And so, many in the administration were caught off guard when Bush informed Scowcroft and Baker the day after the Security Council's historic vote that he wanted to make a last-ditch effort to avoid war. The president proposed sending Baker to Baghdad to meet with Saddam sometime between December 15 and January 15. Although Scowcroft was dubious, Bush and Baker understood that a dramatic effort to avoid war would be useful in getting Congress to authorize the use of military force, a show of unity the president believed desirable. After much wrangling, it was agreed that Baker would meet with Tariq Aziz in Geneva on January 9, 1991. At the meeting, Baker presented a letter for Aziz to deliver to Saddam. Hands shaking, Aziz read the letter and underlined key passages, including, "Unless you withdraw from Kuwait completely and without condition, you will lose more than Kuwait. What is at issue here is not the future of Kuwait—it will be free, its government will be restored—but rather the future of Iraq. The choice is yours to make." At the meeting's seven-hour mark, Baker nodded to the letter now sitting in the middle of the table and asked, "Mr. Minister, is it your intention not to take the letter?" Aziz answered affirmatively, at which point Baker rose and walked out of the room.

On January 14 the House and Senate passed a joint resolution authorizing the use of force to expel Iraq from Kuwait. The vote was 250–183 in the House; 52–47 in the Senate. This vote was difficult for many congressional Democrats. A combination of partisan politics and the stinging legacy of the Vietnam War prevented many from voting in favor of the resolution. Yet, as Pickering observed, the many UN Security Council resolutions "were a strong reason why otherwise reluctant Democratic senators joined in supporting a congressional joint resolution authorizing President Bush to send in U.S. forces."[84] Armed with congressional and United Nations authorizations to use military force, Bush issued the order to commence bombing Iraqi positions in Kuwait and Iraq on January 16. Desert Storm had begun.[85]

CHAPTER 4

Operation Desert Storm

George Bush's decision on October 31, 1990, to more than double the size of the force deployed to Saudi Arabia was an inflection point in the Persian Gulf crisis. The volume of resources Bush agreed to commit was staggering, more than what General Norman Schwarzkopf, the commander of US Central Command, had requested. All told, Bush's decision put roughly 540,000 American military personnel under Schwarzkopf's command, laying to rest the CENTCOM commander's concerns about the feasibility of an offensive military campaign designed to evict Iraq from Kuwait.

The decision to go big was the product of mutual frustrations on the part of both senior military officers and civilian leaders in Washington over how an offensive in Iraq should be conducted. Beginning in mid-August, Schwarzkopf and his CENTCOM team began outlining a potential offensive campaign against Iraqi forces in Kuwait. At the time, the coalition's mission was to deter an Iraqi attack on Saudi Arabia and to repel an invading force should deterrence fail.

On August 16 Schwarzkopf met with Air Force strategist Colonel John Warden III to discuss options for an aerial counterattack should Saddam's forces strike southward. Satisfied with Warden's plan, Schwarzkopf asked Warden for his thoughts on an air component to a larger offensive operation to expel Iraq from Kuwait. Warden offered a target list that included Iraq's command and control systems (including its senior leadership), air defenses, airfields, and critical domestic support infrastructure, as well as Iraq's air defenses in Kuwait. Schwarzkopf believed that a ground campaign would necessarily follow an air campaign and added to Warden's plan the objective of attritting Iraqi combat power in Kuwait by 50 percent.[1] From that conversation the outlines of a sequential air-ground offensive campaign took shape, though the final component, the ground attack phase, was completely undeveloped.[2] In a briefing given to Gen. Colin Powell, Schwarzkopf emphasized that at this point he had no specific ground attack scheme to offer, adding that he "doubted we could come up with a satisfactory one without a whole lot more troops."[3]

Schwarzkopf was confident that US and coalition air forces would ultimately succeed in degrading Iraqi combat power in Kuwait, but he never believed that airpower alone could dislodge the occupying forces. Rather, Schwarzkopf thought that a sizable ground offensive would be needed. Two problems confronted the CENTCOM planning team. First, the president had yet to articulate a clear set of objectives that would give direction to an offensive operation. Vital questions needed to be answered, including whether the eviction of Iraqi forces was sufficient or whether coalition forces needed to plan to take out the regime in Baghdad. Additionally, Schwarzkopf operated under what he considered to be severe force level restrictions. While he and Powell were convinced that coalition forces would be able to successfully defend Saudi Arabia by December, tasking those troops with an offensive mission would court significant risk given the number of Iraqi soldiers, tanks, and artillery pieces in Kuwait. Saddam relieved some of the pressure on Schwarzkopf in mid-September by ordering his forces in Kuwait to assume a defensive posture, a clear indication that he had abandoned the idea of invading Saudi Arabia for the time being. Still, to Schwarzkopf's mind the relatively small number of US and coalition troops available precluded everything but a risky attack.

For two months CENTCOM's planning team worked up an offensive campaign plan employing a single corps-sized contingent of forces from those committed to the defense of Saudi Arabia.[4] "The offensive lacked any element of surprise," Schwarzkopf recalled. "It was a straight-up-the-middle charge right into the teeth of the Iraqi defense." The plan envisioned using all available armored divisions, leaving none in reserve. Should anything go wrong (a near certainty in war), the Iraqis would find ample opportunity to bog coalition forces down, forcing a costly war of attrition favoring the numerically superior occupying power. Despite these drawbacks, Schwarzkopf concluded that "unless the President sent more forces, this was the best possible approach."[5]

Powell told Schwarzkopf on October 6 that he wanted Bush, Dick Cheney, James Baker, and Brent Scowcroft briefed on the evolving plan. The last thing Schwarzkopf wanted was to have what he knew to be a flawed plan scrutinized by senior officials in Washington. He therefore instructed his staff to prepare a detailed presentation covering the air-ground offensive concept and to make it clear that he had serious concerns with the plan. On October 10 the CENTCOM briefers spelled out the air and ground phases to the joint chiefs of staff and Cheney. While the air component was well received, Powell understood immediately why Schwarzkopf objected to having the ground attack phase presented. The plan was, in fact, weak—weaker than it should have been, Powell believed. The chairman recognized that Schwarzkopf was in a bind, that a superior strategy could not be fully developed without additional forces. Yet to Powell's mind, the plan was unimaginative, involving an attack with all US divisions directly into the heart of Iraq's defensive lines in Kuwait. More disturbing was the fact that CENTCOM's scheme made no effort to exploit a known vulnerability in the Iraqi troop disposition, its lightly defended right flank in Kuwait, which was open to both ground and air attack. Finally, to Powell's dismay the CENTCOM's briefers failed to show how their plan would change for the better if additional forces were allocated.[6]

The CENTCOM team repeated its performance the following day, this time for Bush, Scowcroft, Cheney, and Baker. Again, the air campaign drew praise while the ground attack plan came under heavy fire. Scowcroft questioned why a western flanking maneuver hadn't been considered. Powell responded that such a move was logistically unsustainable and would have insufficient mass given the size of the force committed to the Persian Gulf. At that point, the president asked what force level would be required to pull off a more powerful and effective flanking maneuver. Powell answered that an additional corps would do the trick and that such a force could be deployed by January 1.[7]

Scowcroft's assessment of CENTCOM's planning effort was scathing. The briefing "sounded unenthusiastic, delivered by people who didn't want to do the job.... I was appalled with the presentation and afterwards I called Cheney to say I thought we had to do better."[8] Scowcroft's criticism, along with the nickname "General McClellan" that Schwarzkopf earned in Washington after the briefing, were perhaps a bit harsh. Schwarzkopf had, in fact, considered a flanking attack option but rejected it on the grounds that such a scheme was logistically infeasible.[9] In any case, the lack of a viable plan and CENTCOM's inability to reassure leaders in Washington that a sounder approach was forthcoming spurred Cheney and Powell—separately—to find ways of prodding Schwarzkopf in the right direction.

In mid-October, Assistant Secretary of Defense for International Security Affairs Henry Rowen offered Cheney an alternative to the up-the-middle assault plan.[10] Rowen's idea involved inserting one or two American divisions into western Iraq near Baghdad. This component's mission would be to threaten the capital city, divert Iraq's forces northward away from Kuwait, and induce Saddam into conceding Kuwait in exchange for the security of Baghdad. Rowen likened this plan to Gen. Douglas MacArthur's Inchon landing during the Korean War, a bold stroke that forced much of the North Korean army to abandon its attack on the Pusan Perimeter in South Korea.[11] Powell, Schwarzkopf, and Vice Chairman of the Joint Chiefs of Staff David Jeremiah were dead set against Rowen's approach, finding it "almost irresponsible."[12] Rowen's proposal failed to address the principal strategic issue: the destruction of the Iraqi Republican Guard (IRG). Moreover, the plan smacked of Vietnam-era ideas about how force could be used as tools for signaling and bargaining. If force were to be used, both Powell and Schwarzkopf were determined to employ it overwhelmingly.[13] Rowen's plan did have one attribute Cheney found attractive: "it had lit a fire under the military" to infuse the planning effort with more aggression, creativity, and urgency.[14]

With twice as many forces at his disposal, Schwarzkopf's team produced a new plan that would push westward into Iraq and then circle around to hit the Iraqi force in its flanks. Separately, Powell tasked his own staff to produce a plan with a similar axis of advance. The result was an option that pushed further to the west and with more forces than the

CENTCOM scheme. Powell preferred his staff's approach because the CENTCOM plan didn't offer the "roundhouse punch" the army could and should administer.[15] After consulting with Powell, Schwarzkopf directed his group to plan the attack as far to the west as logistics would permit. Throughout November and December, Cheney closely monitored this planning process, receiving fifteen detailed briefings covering every aspect of the evolving campaign plan.[16] Although Cheney's intent was not to micromanage the plan's construction, he was determined "to own it when it's finished," to ensure that the president's political objectives were translated into the coalition's operations and strategy.[17]

The campaign plan that emerged was dubbed "the left hook." In the east, US Marines and Arab coalition partners would enter Kuwait with the goal of fixing Iraqi forces in place, feints designed to distract the Iraqis from the coalition's main attack vector. That component of the plan entailed British, French, and American forces launching an all-out assault from Saudi Arabia far to the west of the Iraq-Kuwait border. The goal was to envelop and destroy the IRG in Iraq and the Iraqi regular army in Kuwait with an overwhelming force.[18] Simultaneously, coalition air power would pummel Iraqi units in the KTO throughout the depth of the battlespace.[19] In a briefing to CENTCOM subordinate commanders, Schwarzkopf emphasized that the IRG was the principal target, or the "center of gravity" in military strategic parlance.[20] "We need to destroy—not attack, not damage, not surround—I want you to *destroy* the Republican Guard. When you're done with them, I don't want them to be an effective fighting force anymore. I don't want them to exist as a military organization."[21]

The goal of destroying (or attritting) a sizable proportion of Iraq's army was a deliberate choice. Yet, alternative strategic and operational approaches were available that could have, at least conceivably, forced the Iraqi military to collapse. Rendering the IRG an ineffective fighting force could have been attempted by an approach known as "maneuver warfare." Whereas attrition warfare seeks to defeat the enemy by annihilating a vital proportion of its forces, maneuver warfare aims to induce psychological paralysis throughout the opponent's military organization. A result of combining speed, flexibility, and surprise, psychological paralysis prevents the opponent from responding effectively to the actions of the force moving deep behind the frontline of the defense. The destruction of the opposing force is not the objective of maneuver warfare because the act of destroying consumes both time and resources. Rather, by concentrating on the enemy's weak points and avoiding its strong points, maneuver warfare seeks to pose repeated, surprising, and seemingly intractable problems for the enemy to solve. In the end, the opponent's military organization collapses from within, preferring surrender to physical destruction.[22] Schwarzkopf was familiar with maneuver warfare theory and with its chief proponent in the United States, John Boyd. Moreover, Cheney had a close association with Boyd going back to his days as a congressman from Wyoming and found his warfighting theories compelling.[23]

Yet, Schwarzkopf's ground attack plan rejected maneuver warfare's emphasis on organizational paralysis as the key to victory. Schwarzkopf believed that the surest route to success was to encircle, and through combined air and ground operations, physically destroy the IRG in what German military theorists evocatively call a "cauldron battle" (*Kesselschlacht*).[24] As the historian Robert Citino observes, Schwarzkopf's plan "seen on a situation map . . . looks very much like the Schlieffen Plan of 1914." The coalition would not engage the IRG with armored columns advancing deep behind the front line of troops. Rather, the plan called for the assembled forces to stretch "as far as the eye could see from north to south," a linear front that would slam into the IRG's flanks "with earthshaking result."[25]

Most importantly, the high mobility attrition-style of fighting in Schwarzkopf's campaign plan served US grand strategic objectives in ways that a maneuver-based approach could not. Chief among the concerns of America's Gulf partners were Saddam's intentions and capabilities after the war. Arab leaders feared the prospect of a war that merely wounded Saddam but left the bulk of his army intact. Saudi Arabia's King Fahd, in fact, concluded early on that his regime's security would be greatly imperiled unless Saddam was "shamefully expelled from Kuwait, or—even better—overthrown."[26]

A war for regime change, however, was not Bush's intent. Determined to use the crisis in the Gulf to bolster the United Nation's collective security function, Bush believed it was imperative that the coalition's war aims strictly adhere to the letter of UN Security Council resolutions, namely the limited objective of ejecting Iraq from Kuwait.[27] To secure and retain frontline Arab states in the international coalition, therefore, the war plan had to have as a top priority the significant reduction of Saddam Hussein's military capabilities. Explaining this objective to Gorbachev in mid-January, Bush maintained that the coalition's "Arab allies would certainly see victory for Saddam if his military was left intact."[28] Schwarzkopf understood this objective clearly, describing it to his subordinates later in February 1991 as inflicting "maximum destruction, *maximum destruction*, on the Iraqi military machine. You are to destroy all war-fighting equipment. Do not just pass it on the battlefield. We don't want the Iraqis coming at us again five years from now."[29]

"Maximum destruction," however, did not mean the total annihilation of Iraq's military. A portion of the IRG had to be spared, American policymakers reasoned, so that postwar Iraq would not be eyed as an easy target by its potentially predatory neighbors, especially Iran. Iraq could not become a "power vacuum (unable to deter or prevent dismemberment by one of its neighbors)," National Security Council staffer Richard Haass wrote in a memo detailing the coalition's war aims.[30] CENTCOM planners thus aimed to destroy Saddam's army south of the Euphrates River, leaving the remainder of his forces north of that point largely untouched. While Saddam's military had to be weakened to the point that the security concerns of America's Arab partners were addressed, Iraq itself had to retain sufficient capabilities after the war to balance against Iranian designs. Striking this balance was seen as critical to ensuring regional stability after the war. In his September 1990 address to Congress, Bush specified two important roles for the United States in the new world order: to deter future aggression and to help America's friends in their own self-defense.[31] CENTCOM's campaign plan aimed to fulfill both objectives.

Incorporating the Arab states' militaries into the campaign was critical for both grand strategic and operational reasons. In terms of grand strategy, Bush sought to construct as broad a military coalition as possible to enhance the legitimacy of the use of force.[32] Arab states' participation in the coalition, moreover, was believed essential to reviving the UN's collective security function in the post–Cold War era. "The Arab forces, in this war, were absolutely critical to its success," commander of British forces Lieut. Gen. Peter de la Billière recalled. "Without them and without having them along, then we would not have been welcome. If we had won a military battle, we'd have lost a political peace."[33] Operationally, CENTCOM planners wanted Arab partners to participate because they added needed mass to the invading force and because of the niche capabilities and critical functions their militaries offered.[34]

Ensuring Arab partners' participation proved to be challenging, however. Determining whether, how, and where their armies would be used wasn't simply a matter of military necessity. More important were the coalition members' political and diplomatic sensitivities. Schwarzkopf had to navigate three issues to keep Arab states in the coalition. The first was the widely held principle that although it was acceptable for an Arab army to come to the aid of a fellow Arab nation, attacking another Arab country was not. This meant that CENTCOM could employ Arab armies for the attack into Kuwait, but not for the left hook component into Iraq. To accommodate this stipulation, CENTCOM's plan entailed two axes of advance into Kuwait: one comprising US Marines and a Saudi taskforce charged with tying up Iraqi forces and then encircling Kuwait City, and another comprising a pan-Arab component that would attack further west into Kuwait to cut off the Iraqi army's main supply route northwest of the capital city.[35] Employing Arab armies solely in Kuwait reduced the political pressure on leaders in the region and enabled more states to participate in a war that many in the region opposed.[36]

Second, despite Saudi Arabia's extensive cooperation with the United States in the crisis, it was Egypt's decision to participate in the offensive to liberate Kuwait that had the greatest influence on Arab states' calculations.[37] "The entire Arab world was watching to see whether Cairo would join the offensive," Schwarzkopf recalled. On January 25, Hosni Mubarak publicly stated that his country would help liberate Kuwait.[38] Yet, Cairo refused to allow its forces to participate in an attack on Iraq. Schwarzkopf assigned them the difficult mission of breaching Iraqi defenses in Kuwait, a task for which the Egyptian army was particularly well suited.[39]

Third, some Arab states refused to subordinate their forces to an

American commander. Syria, a country designated as a state-sponsor of terrorism by the United States, was one such country. Although its forces had already been subordinated to a Saudi commander, on December 31 officials in Damascus announced that the Syrian army would not join the offensive into Kuwait. This decision posed an immediate problem because Syrian armor had been assigned the job of protecting the flanks of the highly prized Egyptian force tasked with breaching Iraqi fixed positions in Kuwait. Without Syria's participation, the Egyptians would be outgunned and likely incapable of completing their mission. Schwarzkopf and the commander of the joint Arab forces Khalid bin Sultan eventually devised a solution: Syrian tank units would be used as a mobile reserve force for the Egyptian advance, a follow-on force that would come to the Egyptian forces' aid if they were attacked by the Iraqi defenders. Syrian forces—which were neither under US command nor employed in a direct attack on another Arab state—would participate in the liberation of Kuwait after all.[40]

From Air War to Ground War

Desert Storm began on January 17 with an air campaign that initially aimed at decapitating the Iraqi regime. The first phase of the air war, dubbed Instant Thunder, sought to "kill, overthrow, or isolate Saddam Hussein and his regime or use the threat of these events to compel Saddam to withdraw from Kuwait." Instant Thunder's principal architect, Col. John Warden, believed Saddam could be compelled to abandon Kuwait by the bombing of critical strategic targets in Iraq. Warden's plan largely ignored Iraqi targets in Kuwait, focusing instead on the connections among Iraq's leaders, the army, and key economic and industrial nodes.[41] The operation failed to achieve its intended results. Although coalition air power destroyed virtually all of Warden's targets in the first six days, the decapitation strategy did not dent Saddam's resolve to keep Kuwait firmly in his grip.[42] Instant Thunder had another problem: it was designed to achieve only one of the two main objectives of the war effort—Iraq's withdrawal from Kuwait. As we have seen, senior US officials also wanted to substantially degrade Iraqi combat power. On the seventh day of the war, coalition air power turned decisively to that mission.

Iraq's army was deployed in a defense-in-depth scheme comprising three echelons. The first was a defensive screen from west to east along the Saudi-Kuwait border and south to north along the Kuwaiti coastline. This frontline deployment was made up of Iraq's least trained, equipped, and motived forces. Behind this line in Kuwait were heavy formations of Iraq's regular army, which were in turn reinforced by Iraq's best trained, equipped, and motivated force, the IRG positioned in southeastern Iraq. The IRG's mission was to serve as a mobile reserve force that would plug any gaps created by advancing coalition forces. Saddam's plan was to channel the invading forces crossing the border into kill zones, to defend the Kuwaiti coast against a possible amphibious attack, and ultimately produce more casualties than the coalition could stomach.[43]

Two assumptions underpinned Saddam's strategy. The first was that a ground war suited Iraq because the United States was too weakly resolved to sustain a long, bloody war. The second was that Iraq's western flank didn't need robust protection because the vast featureless desert would pose insurmountable navigation problems for a mobile ground force. Saddam failed to understand just how vulnerable his troops were to advanced Western airpower. The coalition's theater bombing strategy sought to sap the morale of the occupying Iraqi army by disabling its logistical support network and to destroy any maneuvering Iraqi forces in the KTO. Sometime in early February, US F-111 crews returning to base noticed that dug-in Iraqi tanks could also be detected by the Aardvark's targeting instruments right as dusk set in—when the metallic skin of Iraqi armor cooled slower than the surrounding sand. Soon thereafter, coalition air power began pounding Iraqi tanks in fixed positions, a practice known at the time as "tank plinking."[44]

Saddam had two reactions at the start of the air campaign. The first was to try driving a wedge in the coalition by inducing Israel to enter the war. Beginning on January 17, Iraqi Scud missiles were fired at Israel, most striking well wide of their intended targets. Nevertheless, the political impact of Saddam's decision was explosive. On January 28 Powell, Cheney, and Deputy Undersecretary of Defense for Policy Paul Wolfowitz met with a senior Israeli delegation in the Pentagon. The American defense officials were told that Israel planned to intervene in the war to put an end to the Iraqi threat. Deputy Chief of Staff of the Israel Defense Force General Ehud Barak told Powell that despite the Scud's shoddiness, Saddam's missiles were terrorizing the Israeli population. Barak was concerned that, while Saddam had so far lobbed only conventional munitions, he would soon decide to attack with chemical or biological warheads. "It is hard for Israelis to have others risk their lives in our defense," Barak told Powell. "We want in."[45]

From the start, Saddam sought to portray himself as the leader of a pan-Arab bulwark against imperialism and Zionism. If he had successfully manipulated Israel into joining the war, his message would have been more widely embraced in the region, putting significant pressure on the leaders of Arab states in the coalition to abandon the effort. Describing the danger, Scowcroft recalled that "the attack was a shrewd attempt to split the Arab allies from the coalition, either by directly provoking an Israeli military response or by gathering support among radical Arabs."[46]

The Bush administration took several steps to shore up the cohesion of the coalition in these circumstances. Additional Patriot missile defense batteries were sent to protect Israeli cities from incoming Scuds. At great risk, British and American special operations forces were deployed deep into western Iraq to search for missile launch sites.[47] Most significantly, senior US officials prevailed on Schwarzkopf to divert one-third of all air combat sorties to the Scud hunt in western Iraq. This level of effort, to Schwarzkopf's mind, made little sense because most of the targets provided by the Israelis had already been identified and hit by coalition air power. "We'll do what you tell us," Schwarzkopf told Powell, "but just to have bombs falling out of the sky defies military logic."[48] That may have been true, but Bush's political objective of maintaining a cohesive coalition called for this level of inefficiency in military activity.[49] To keep the Israelis out of the war, Bush told Israeli prime minister Yitzhak Shamir that there was nothing more that Israel could do to mitigate the Scud threat than what the coalition was already doing. To make good on that statement, coalition air power had to be seen going the extra mile. The coalition's Scud hunt in the air and on the ground, coupled with a lengthy stay in Tel Aviv during the Scud attacks by Wolfowitz and Deputy Secretary of State Lawrence Eagleburger, convinced Shamir to remain out of the war.[50]

Saddam's second response to the air campaign was to try to shorten it by goading the coalition into launching a ground invasion. Reflecting his experiences in the eight-year war with Iran, Saddam's theory of victory was that an enemy would likely succumb if it were aggressively and decisively challenged.[51] Further, Saddam thought the Americans would fold quickly because they lacked the Iranians' determination to fight under brutal conditions. "Only we are willing to accept casualties, the Americans are not," Saddam insisted. "The American people are weak."[52] Critically, Saddam didn't believe that his military had to destroy the coalition to win the war. All he had to do was get the United States committed to a ground war early on and then impose an unacceptable level of cost on its military.[53] Content to prolong the air campaign, however, the coalition wasn't playing ball.

Taking matters into his own hands, Saddam ordered an excursion to take Khafji, a coastal Saudi town near the Kuwaiti border. Due to its exposure to Iraqi artillery in Kuwait, Khafji had already been evacuated and was only lightly defended. From Saddam's perspective, it was the ideal target. On January 29 three Iraqi divisions headed to Khafji, two attempting to distract coalition air power, the third tasked with taking the town. The coalition's response was decisive. Not only were Iraqi units obliterated from the sky by US aircraft but the short-lived ground battle afforded the Saudi army the chance to win a quick victory and boost its morale as a fighting force.[54] Lasting a mere two days, the battle for Khafji exposed the vulnerabilities of Iraq's maneuvering army to sophisticated US targeting systems on board aircraft that enjoyed complete command of the air.[55] The battle also showed that small-scale cross-border raids were not going to force the coalition to abandon its theater bombing campaign. The battle likely had the opposite effect because it illustrated that Saddam's army still had the ability to conduct complex multidivisional operations. By the end of January, coalition commanders saw that they still had their work cut out for them; they had yet to conclude that the time was right for the ground campaign to commence.

For the next three weeks, coalition air strikes continued unrelentingly in Iraq and Kuwait. Saddam could do little but watch as his army's combat power was steadily eroded, both in terms of the numbers of tanks, armored personnel carriers, artillery pieces, and troops lost and of his ability to exercise command and control. To be sure, Iraq's army retained much of its capability by the time the ground war commenced. According to a CIA estimate conducted after the war, coalition air power attritted 43 percent of Iraq's armored vehicles in the KTO—a large percentage, but not enough to guarantee a coalition victory.[56] Despite punishing attacks on Iraq's command, control, communications, and intelligence system, once the ground war started Iraqi commanders were able to identify threats to their position and have their subordinates move to defend against them.[57] Still, Saddam understood that as long as the air campaign continued, he could do nothing to prevent the steady decimation of his forces.

US officials' willingness to prolong the air campaign ended in mid-February due to an unwelcomed diplomatic gambit launched by Mikhail Gorbachev. Gorbachev's goal was to find a political solution to the conflict before the start of the ground campaign. Ever since the passing of UNSCR 678 on November 29, 1990, his domestic and international standing had become untenable. Gorbachev's conception of the new world order did not entail the use of force to resolve disputes among states. "We had entered the new era," Gorbachev lamented, "announced as the era of the new world order, to the thunder of cannons—not the best accomplishment."[58] His adviser Anatoly Chernyaev maintained that the Soviet leader was dedicated to replacing the "tried and true" methods of force with the "moral factor" in interstate relations.[59] While he believed that coercive diplomacy could work against Saddam, Gorbachev held that force should not be used to compel Iraq to accept America's maximalist demands. As Chief of the General Staff of the Soviet Armed Forces Mikhail Moiseyev summarized to Bush in October 1990, "The position of the USSR and the President is clear. From the first day we have supported the position against Hussein. Annexation is impermissible. But it is not possible to use arms for this. Our idea of revolution [in international affairs] is that it should be peaceful without using arms."[60] Yet, Gorbachev's influence with the international coalition lessened substantially once he assented to use "all necessary means" to force Iraq from Kuwait after the January 15 deadline. Having made his principal political contribution, and with neither a military nor an economic stake in the coalition, Gorbachev discovered that his counsel had less impact in Washington.

Domestically, Gorbachev was under unremitting pressure from both sides of the political spectrum. Liberals complained that Gorbachev's reforms had been incremental and partial, at best. More ominously, conservatives, including the so-called power ministries (the KGB and the Ministries of Defense and Interior), charged that Gorbachev's radical reforms had produced chaos in the country. Moreover, Gorbachev had capitulated to the United States time and again, leading to a situation where America would be free to dominate the Middle East if Saddam were to be politically humiliated and militarily weakened. On top of it all, citizens in the Baltic states were agitating for a break with the Soviet Union, a situation, the hardliners insisted, that demanded a firm response—which came on January 13 when a crackdown on demonstrators in Vilnius killed fifteen people.[61]

Spurred by both principle and pressure, Gorbachev took a hard right turn by accruing more powers for the office of the presidency, an act that prompted Foreign Minister Eduard Shevardnadze to resign in protest. Gorbachev also sent his special envoy Yevgeny Primakov to Baghdad to try to find some arrangement with Saddam that would avoid a ground war.[62] On February 12 Primakov arrived in Iraq and urged Saddam to announce his willingness to leave Kuwait in exchange for a ceasefire, a deal, Baker noted, "Primakov had no authority to offer and which was unacceptable on its face." Shevardnadze's successor as foreign minister, Alexander Bessmertnykh, called Baker on February 15 to say that Saddam was exhibiting "encouraging behavior," an indication that he was coming to terms with the gravity of the situation he was confronting. Gorbachev followed up with a letter to Bush stating that Iraq's foreign minister Tariq Aziz would travel to Moscow in the coming days to continue working toward an end to the conflict on peaceful terms. Gorbachev closed the letter stating that "it would not be desirable to conduct any massive ground operations, if they are being planned, during the period of the Moscow talks." Three days later, the Soviets informed the Americans that the meeting with Aziz had achieved a breakthrough. According to the draft terms, Iraq would signal its willingness to proceed with an unconditional withdrawal from Kuwait one day after a cease-fire was implemented. Gorbachev also promised Aziz that the Soviet Union would demand that the UN deal with "the whole complex of Middle

East issues and conflicts, including the question of regional security."[63]

Bush rejected Gorbachev's proposal on February 19. Wary of Saddam's duplicity, Baker told Bessmertnykh that a withdrawal had to *begin* with a cease-fire, not come after the shooting had stopped. Bush added specificity on this point in a letter to Gorbachev, stating that a cease-fire would not even be considered until Iraq began a "massive" withdrawal that took no more than ninety-six hours to complete.[64] On the twenty-second, Gorbachev informed the White House that Saddam had agreed to an unconditional and immediate withdrawal that would begin one day after a cease-fire and would take approximately three weeks to accomplish. Gorbachev also highlighted that he had dropped the link between Iraq's decision and an international effort to redress the political and security issues in the broader region. Again, Bush rejected these terms. Bush saw two problems with Gorbachev's most recent proffer. First, the three-week timetable for withdrawal would permit the bulk of Saddam's heavy weapons to be returned safely to Iraq, an unacceptable outcome for the future of regional stability.[65] Second, Saddam had just started torching Kuwait's oilfields, an act of wanton destruction and environmental degradation. "This man will do anything," Bush told Gorbachev. "They set the oilfields afire. We cannot accept that."[66]

Ultimately, Gorbachev's diplomacy to avert a ground campaign was counterproductive. To avoid being presented with a deal that traded Kuwaiti sovereignty for the security of the bulk of Saddam's army, senior US officials now sought to launch the ground war as quickly as possible. During a visit to Saudi Arabia on February 8–10, Cheney and Powell were told by Schwarzkopf that the ground war would be ready to launch on February 21. Yet on the thirteenth, Schwarzkopf called Powell to tell him that the start date had to be pushed back to February 24 due to Gen. Walter Boomer's concerns about the penetrability of the defensive thicket that US Marines would confront in Kuwait. Although Powell thought Schwarzkopf was being overly cautious and that the CENTCOM commander had lost sight of the strategic role of the Marines' attack (to fix Iraqi units in place, not to penetrate deep into Kuwait), the Joint Chiefs' chairman agreed to take the recommendation to Cheney, who subsequently elicited an agreement from Bush to the postponement.[67]

Bush wasn't pleased about the delay, but he wasn't going to directly challenge the military judgment of his combatant commander. Rather, Bush's tack was subtle. Describing his approach in his diary entry for February 18, Bush wrote,

> The meter is ticking. Gosh darn it, I wish Powell and Cheney were ready to go right now. But they aren't, and I'm not going to push them, even though these next few days are fraught with difficulty. Little turns of diplomatic mischief, but I will not order the military to go until they say they're ready. . . . I want to have a meeting with Cheney, Powell, Baker, and all our people at 4:30 in the Oval Office. . . . Maybe I can probe there to see how ready we are.[68]

Notwithstanding Bush's hesitance to challenge Schwarzkopf's judgement, the president's probing was magnified down the line. In a phone call to Schwarzkopf later that day, Powell said that "the National Security Council is saying we may need to attack a little early," giving Schwarzkopf until the next day to offer his judgment. Schwarzkopf responded that an attack on the twenty-second was not possible unless Washington was willing to accept "a whole lot more casualties." Powell informed Schwarzkopf that the administration was afraid that the Gorbachev-Aziz agreement would become a reality. Nevertheless, Schwarzkopf insisted that the twenty-fourth remain the deadline. To the senior commanders in Saudi Arabia, the administration's determination to push the deadline up made little sense. Major General Bob Johnson, for example, expressed his frustration, stating, "The Soviets are talking about getting us exactly what we asked for, and we summarily turned them down."[69]

Tensions between Powell and Schwarzkopf boiled over on February 20 when the CENTCOM commander informed the chairman that, due to an ominous weather forecast, the ground attack might have to be delayed again. Powell responded,

> Ten days ago you told me the 21st. Then you wanted the 24th. Now you're asking for the 26th. I've got a President and a Secretary of Defense on my back. They've got a bad Russian peace proposal they are trying to dodge. You've got to give me a better case for postponement. I don't think you understand the pressure I'm under.

In a volcanic retort, Schwarzkopf complained, "You're giving me political reasons why you don't want to tell the President not to do something militarily unsound."[70] The CENTCOM commander had a point: at the behest of his civilian bosses, Powell was urging Schwarzkopf to launch the offensive at a particular time based not on military factors but on political calculations. Yet, the opening of the ground war *was* a thoroughly political act, one that had to be attuned as much to the ongoing diplomatic activity as to military considerations. This episode of political-military tension was resolved an hour later when Schwarzkopf phoned Powell to tell him the weather forecast had changed for the better. The twenty-fourth was a suitable day for the start of the ground war after all.

While the president and his senior advisers were determined to stymie Gorbachev's diplomacy to avoid the ground war, Bush was not interested in isolating the Soviet leader. "I don't want to take this deal," Powell recalled Bush saying. "But I don't want to stiff Gorbachev, not after he's come this far with us."[71] Rather than reject Gorbachev's initiative outright, Bush countered with a proposal that made Gorbachev feel valued but also put Saddam in a bind. The United States would propose "a procedure by which we can avert a ground campaign and bring the war to an end," Baker explained to Gorbachev on February 22, adding somewhat gratuitously, "In effect, this builds on what you have done." US terms were that Iraq had to begin a large-scale withdrawal from Kuwait by 12:00 on February 23 and complete it in one week. Additionally, Iraq had to evacuate its forces from Kuwait City and remove its prepared defenses in Kuwait and along its border with Saudi Arabia within the first forty-eight hours of the withdrawal. To Gorbachev, these terms appeared—perhaps by design—too onerous for Saddam to accept.[72] "Where does our priority lie in putting a final touch on this settlement?" Gorbachev asked Bush. "Is it a political approach or the continuation of military operations and the escalation to ground operations?"[73] Unmoved by Gorbachev's entreaties, Bush insisted that Saddam's invasion of Kuwait necessitated a firm response. Bush's position was that Saddam "could withdraw in a minute if he wanted" and that to let him off the hook would undermine deterrence against aggression in the new world order.[74] In the end, Saddam allowed the February 23 deadline to lapse. The coalition's ground campaign began at 4:00 a.m. Riyadh time the following day.

War Termination

Complications to the coalition's war plan emerged almost immediately. Again, the objective of the Marines and the Arab taskforce was to fix in place frontline Iraqi troops and to lure in supporting regular army and IRG forces closer to the point of contact. The Iraqi army would be destroyed once it was caught between the hammer of the US VII and XVIII corps and the anvil of the Marines and Arab units.[75] The problem with this plan was that the weeks-long air campaign and the ill-fated Iraqi foray to Khafji had broken much of their army. Rather than fixing frontline Iraqi troops in place, the Marines sliced through Iraq's defenses. Sensing the danger, Iraqi heavy divisions turned and fled instead of moving into the trap the coalition laid for it. "The Marine attack acted like a piston pushing them out [of Kuwait]," Michael Gordon explained. "The Iraqis began to flee, and the war quickly turned into a foot race." The US VII Corps in western Saudi Arabia, whose mission it was to engage and destroy the IRG in Iraq, was set to depart the day after the Marines attack. Yet, the accelerated timetable prevented General Fred Franks from engaging the IRG at the optimal time.[76]

The Twenty-Fourth Mechanized Division under Maj. Gen. Barry McCaffery assessed the situation accurately and pressed the attack along the Euphrates. Meanwhile, the 101st Airborne Division commanded by Maj. Gen. J. H. Binford Peay III made plans to airlift a brigade north of the river to destroy any units that managed to escape. In Kuwait, Lieutenant General Boomer, whose forces had reached the Iraq border, phoned Schwarzkopf's headquarters to say that he was prepared to chase the fleeing Iraqi heavy divisions before they could leave the theater.[77] Schwarzkopf's division commanders had devised on the fly a plan that stood a good chance of achieving the coalition's objective of destroying Saddam's army south of the Euphrates. Schwarzkopf, however, ordered his forces to sit tight. Political developments, once again, affected how military force was used.

On the third day of the ground war, Iraqi units fleeing Kuwait found themselves pinned by US air power on Multa Ridge north of Kuwait City. As they suffered blistering aerial attacks, the scene was soon dubbed the "Highway of Death." Media outlets had not yet acquired photos of the carnage, but officials in Washington knew that CNN would soon get visual evidence of the battle and make it public. Bush feared the political fallout would be significant, possibly even fatal to the coalition. America would look like it was piling on after the outcome of the war was all but certain.[78] The administration was sensitive to the effects that international condemnation could have on the coalition's cohesion. Weeks prior, US aircraft had unintentionally killed hundreds of Iraqi civilians hiding in the Amiriyah air raid bunker in Baghdad. Criticism of the attack came not just from Arab leaders supporting Saddam but also from leaders of coalition member states, including Italy, Sweden, and Spain, who attempted to force a Security Council vote to end the war.[79]

Powell, who had already discussed with Schwarzkopf the military conditions for terminating the war, put the case for ending war early to Bush in ethical terms. "We presently hold the moral high ground. We could lose it by fighting past the 'rational calculation'.... As a professional soldier, I honored the warrior's code. 'We don't want to be seen as killing for the sake of killing, Mr. President'." Powell told Bush that "we're within the window of success" and that based on his conversation with Schwarzkopf, "I expect by sometime tomorrow the job will be done, and I'll probably be bringing you a recommendation to stop the fighting." Bush responded, "If that's the case, why not end it today?" Powell said that he needed to speak to Schwarzkopf, who would confer with his field commanders. At that point, Powell reports, none of Bush's civilian advisers and none of the Joint Chiefs of Staff objected to the idea of ending the war after one hundred hours of ground fighting.[80] Scowcroft recalled that the images from the Highway of Death were important in the president's war-termination decision. "We did not want to look like butchers who were bent on revenge by slaughtering people."[81]

Although Schwarzkopf reported that a decision to suspend hostilities early would allow some IRG tank units to escape destruction, Powell maintains that "no one felt that what we had heard changed the basic equation. The back of the Iraqi army had been broken. What was left of it was retreating north."[82] Yet, there was significant concern among

Schwarzkopf's field commanders and some officials in Washington about the premature ending of the war.[83] Many of them feared that as a result of their not continuing the war for an additional fifth day, a significant number of IRG units south of the Euphrates would survive and join the roughly twenty divisions north of the river.[84] In fact, 842 Iraqi tanks and 1,412 armored vehicles (half of the IRG's equipment and 70 percent of its personnel) escaped back to Iraq after the ceasefire.[85] Headquarters units were able to make their way back as well, enabling the quick reconstitution of the force in response to the Shia uprisings that occurred soon after the war.[86] Despite these risks, on February 27 Bush decided to suspend hostilities the next day at 5:00 a.m. Riyadh time, declaring on national television, "Kuwait is liberated. Iraq's army is defeated. Our military objectives are met."

On March 3 Schwarzkopf met with Iraqi general Sultan Hasheem Ahmad at Safwan to formalize terms of a cease-fire. Acting with minimal instructions from Washington, Schwarzkopf detailed the coalition's demands pertaining to the return of prisoners of war, the fate of Kuwaiti nationals in Iraq, and the demarcation line between the combatants. The Iraqi delegation agreed to each of Schwarzkopf's demands. General Ahmad then stated, "We would like to fly helicopters to carry officials of our government in areas where roads and bridges are out. This has nothing to do with the frontline. This is inside Iraq." Finding this a reasonable request, Schwarzkopf stated, "As long as it is not over the part we are in, that is absolutely no problem," adding that this provision applied only to helicopters, not fighters and bombers. Making sure he understood, Ahmad clarified, "You mean helicopters that are armed can fly in Iraqi skies..." Schwarzkopf concurred. In the following weeks, those helicopters would be used to brutally suppress the Shia uprising. Even still, Schwarzkopf maintains that grounding the gunships would have mattered little because most of the government's attacks against the Shia were conducted by tanks and artillery.[87]

American war aims in the Gulf War were limited by numerous UN Security Council resolutions designed to expel Iraq from Kuwait. Abiding by those strict limits allowed Bush to construct an international coalition of countries that together condemned Iraq's aggression and worked in concert to restore Kuwaiti sovereignty. The destruction of

Iraq's military capability was not, however, a stipulation of those resolutions. Rather, reducing Saddam's military capacity was an American objective, one that was adopted to assuage the security concerns of frontline Arab states. By the time of the Safwan meeting, Saddam's forces were clearly defeated, and Iraq had been forced to retreat from Kuwait. While Saddam retained a considerable conventional force, prolonging the war appeared to US policymakers to be freighted with political cost and risk. Few in the administration believed that Saddam would survive the war, moreover, anticipating that he would either be ousted in a coup or overthrown by a popular uprising. When that uprising began in early March, Saddam used his remaining forces to kill thousands of Kurds and Shia in Iraq's north and south, respectively. Not wanting to be drawn into an internal Iraqi conflict, Bush decided not to intervene.[88] Saddam's ability to threaten his neighbors may have been diminished for the time being, but he retained the willingness and ability to brutalize his own population.

The uprisings against Saddam and their suppression resulted in the deaths of thousands and the displacement of over two million Iraqis. The return of many IRG armor units to Iraq, and the permission Schwarzkopf gave to Ahmad to fly armed helicopters over Iraqi territory, made Saddam's suppression campaign easier. But even without those military assets, Saddam had at his disposal multiple army divisions north of the Euphrates that had not been committed to the fighting. These units were likely sufficient to crush the Kurdish and Shia uprisings. Could the coalition have devised a way to prevent these atrocities while retaining popular legitimacy throughout Desert Shield and Desert Storm?

According to US ambassador to the United Nations Thomas Pickering, the answer is yes. In December 1990 the US mission to the UN proposed the creation of a series of limited armament zones in Iraq that would have been created immediately after the fighting had stopped. "This would begin with a two-hundred-plus-kilometer area in southwestern Iraq, bordering on the populated areas of Anbar Province, free of all Iraqi forces and monitored by the UN. Successive zones would include those limited in armor, artillery, air defense, and so on. A no-fly zone would have been a clear advantage."[89] The two-hundred-kilometer zone was vastly greater than the ten-kilometer zone that was ultimately agreed to in UNSCR 687 and would have given the coalition—with the UN's blessing—much greater capacity to prevent the atrocities that followed. When the proposal to create these limited armament zones resurfaced shortly after the Safwan meeting, however, the US military was quick to shoot it down. "Well we pushed it hard, Baker said he pushed it," Pickering recalled. "It was killed by the military, I think principally General Schwarzkopf, in part because he didn't understand it and two he thought it was going to involve a big effort on the part of the United States military to have to impose this and or to man it."[90] To Pickering's mind, the United States' failure to think through the requirements and process of the termination of the war amounted to a huge missed opportunity, one that would have significant consequences for America's role in the Gulf for years to come.

Compared to how the Bush administration marshalled an international coalition to confront Saddam, planned the air and ground campaigns, and waged war against Iraq, the war termination period stands out as being poorly conceived and sloppily executed. From the point at which the decision was made to confront Iraqi aggression in early August 1990 to the time when initial reports from the Highway of Death made their way to Washington on February 27, 1991, Bush's decision-making process was a model of efficiency and effectiveness. The core of that system was an empowered National Security Council staff led by a team of skilled and trusted professionals. Under Scowcroft and Gates, the NSC staff knitted together myriad diplomatic and military policies and worked to ensure that Bush's objectives served as the focal point of US national security policy. Bush's senior team—Baker, Cheney, and Scowcroft—were themselves dedicated to the president's objectives and sought to instill an ethos of cooperation into interagency relations. The result was a decision-making system that provided senior officials with a wealth of high-quality information, verified that decisions translated into appropriate actions, and ensured that Bush's strategic objectives oriented American policy.[91]

This system broke down due in large measure to the military success of the coalition's air and ground campaigns. The effectiveness of the bombing campaign and the inability of the Iraqi army to obstruct the coalition's ground assault generated a rapid and decisive cratering of Iraq's military endurance. The Iraqi military collapsed with surprising speed, and Bush's decision-making system struggled to keep up with events on the ground. A once well-managed, methodical routine devolved into an ad hoc process that responded to events without the due diligence the administration had shown itself capable of conducting. This conclusion finds widespread support among former administration officials. Reflecting on decision-making at the time of the war's end, NSC staffer Richard Haass remarked, "It must be said that U.S. policy making during this period was ragged. There is simply no other word for it."[92] Pickering, too, recalled that "the notion of an early collapse was not so easy to envisage. . . . We underestimated the rapidity of victory and the completeness of it and we did little to prepare for that circumstances [sic] or indeed the circumstances that would result from a long military effort to expel the Iraqis from Kuwait. We didn't do war termination well."[93] In his memoirs, Schwarzkopf recalls the interminable delays from Washington as he prepared for the Safwan meeting. Preparing the terms of reference document required coordination among the White House, State Department, Defense Department, Moscow, and Baghdad. The "various bureaucracies were having trouble keeping up with [the] pace of events," Schwarzkopf concluded.[94] Ultimately, the Bush administration gave inadequate thought and preparation to converting favorable military outcomes into its political objectives.[95] How this failure impacted American grand strategy will be the focus of the final chapter.

CHAPTER 5

War and Statecraft in the Post–Cold War Era

Notwithstanding America's diplomatic and military successes in the Persian Gulf War, the aftermath of the conflict revealed an international system at odds with many of George Bush's strategic beliefs. Part of the problem was that while Iraq's military had been soundly beaten by the international coalition that Bush worked assiduously to construct, Saddam Hussein did not appear chastened in defeat. A wily and brutal dictator, there was little Saddam would not do retain his grip on power. Although the UN mandate prevented the United States from seeking regime change in 1991, Bush administration officials wanted Saddam to fall; many expected his ouster in light of his military's disastrous performance in the war.[1] Bush encouraged both Iraq's people and its military to take matters into their own hands and topple the Baathist regime. "There's another way for the bloodshed to stop, and that is for the Iraqi military and the Iraqi people to take matters into their own hands and force Saddam Hussein, the dictator, to step aside," Bush stated on February 15. "We have no argument with the people of Iraq. Our differences are with that brutal dictator in Baghdad."[2] Whether the president's words carried much weight with these audiences remains in dispute. Nonetheless, Iraq's Kurdish and Shia communities rose and challenged Saddam's rule. Saddam's answer was vicious.

In response to Saddam's suppression campaign, the UN Security Council passed resolution 688 on April 5, 1991, which for the first time in its history made the humanitarian treatment of groups within states a matter of the international organization's concern. The Security Council justified its action on the grounds that Kurdish refugee flows threatened Turkey's security and political stability. The UN's condemnation of Iraq's actions paved the way for Operation Provide Comfort, launched on April 7, which initially supplied food, medicine, and other materials needed by the suffering Kurdish population. The refugees remained vulnerable to Saddam's military, however, and Operation Provide Comfort soon expanded to include a military component. Using UNSCR 688 as a predicate, the United States, Great Britain, and France instituted a no-fly zone over northern Iraq.[3] This action, a violation of Iraqi sovereignty, proved to be transformative for the United Nations—and for American grand strategy. Elected in late 1991, Secretary General Boutros Boutros-Ghali pledged to reform the UN by providing the Security Council with resources to better enforce its resolutions and keep the peace in states riven by internal conflicts.[4] Reflecting the international community's willingness to wade into states' internal affairs on humanitarian grounds, the United States and its allies didn't seek a separate Security Council resolution when they jointly established a second no-fly zone over southern Iraq in August 1992.

The imposition of the two no-fly zones over Iraq was a reasonable response to the security threats facing Iraq's Shia and Kurdish populations. These operations, moreover, reflected the international community's appetite to redress gross human right violations. Yet, the challenges Bush confronted after the Gulf War were not the type that his New World Order grand strategy was designed to address. As discussed in chapter 2, Bush's strategic beliefs were traditional to the extent that he saw state-based aggression as the principal threat to international peace and stability. In the new era, however, violent internal conflicts became the primary threat to international stability.[5] While horrifying in their consequences, the national security implications of these conflicts were unclear to officials in Washington.[6] As Yugoslavia disintegrated, for example, Bush passed the buck, preferring instead a European solution to the problem. Absent strong American leadership, the war in Bosnia raged without resolution until 1995.[7] Bush's grand strategic goal of deterring regional interstate aggression quickly lost saliency. Instead, the administration found itself enmeshed in Iraq's internal politics, with few good options. And while the international community went along with the implementation of the no-fly zones, the seeds of great power discord had been planted. However reluctant the United States was to intervene on behalf of repressed populations, Russian and Chinese leaders were uncomfortable with the precedent that had been set.[8]

Bush decided to end the war after four days of ground combat based on Colin Powell's moral appeal. When placed on the scales, the ethical prohibition against slaughtering defenseless and surrendering soldiers outweighed the strategic objective of attritting the Iraqi army south of the Euphrates River. Due to the raggedness of Bush's decision-making process at this point in the war, the ceasefire negotiations held at Safwan and the determination by senior military officers to vacate Iraq expeditiously turned an otherwise noble choice into tragedy.[9] The administration was left with scant resources to effectively and humanely enforce compliance of the terms imposed on Iraq by Security Council resolution 687. Dubbed "the mother of all resolutions," UNSCR 687 imposed a comprehensive set of demands on Iraq, including the establishment of a demilitarized zone in Iraqi territory, the prohibition of weapons of mass destruction with a robust monitoring system to ensure compliance, and the obligation of reparations payments to Kuwait.[10] As UNSCR 687 was passed after coalition forces left Iraq, the only coercive instrument available to ensure Baghdad's compliance with these terms was the economic sanctions the resolution kept in place.

The retention of the sanctions regime quickly became politically contentious because of the humanitarian disaster in Iraq caused by the war itself. The UN's Under-Secretary General Martii Ahtisaari, who led an observer mission to Iraq in March, reported that "nothing that we had seen or read had quite prepared us for the particular form of devastation which has now befallen the country." The war "wrought near-apocalyptic results upon the economic infrastructure of what had been, until January 1991, a rather highly urbanized and mechanized society." The report stood in marked contrast to the relatively light damage done to Iraq's civilian infrastructure that the US military officials reported through the bombing campaign. In May of that year, a team from Harvard University conducted a study that estimated that at least 170,000 children under five years of age would die from disease if the humanitarian crisis went unaddressed. Then in July, the UN secretary general's executive delegate for the humanitarian crisis in Iraq reported that the country was generating a mere 25 percent of the electrical power compared to prewar levels, that many Iraqis lacked access to clean water, and that cholera and typhoid outbreaks were occurring due to the raw sewage that was flowing in the streets of some cities. Finally, economic sanctions were exacerbating food shortages and threatening to "cause massive starvation throughout the country."[11]

The sanctions regime remained in place, although several states (including China, India, and Cuba) were uneasy about its consequences. The Bush administration pressed to retain the sanctions for two reasons. First, sanctions afforded the international community a plausible alternative to the use of military force in the new world order. Second, the administration lacked an alternative to address what it came to understand as the key problem—Saddam's grip on power. Because a direct American attack on Saddam was out of the question, Bush directed the CIA to create the conditions for Saddam's ouster. But removing Saddam indirectly by a coup or popular uprising would take time. In the moment, the administration sought an agreement that would allow Iraq to sell oil on international markets to purchase food and other humanitarian supplies. Saddam rejected this proposal, however, on the grounds that it violated Iraqi sovereignty. While the Security Council was largely united in condemning Iraq for the failure of the proposed oil-for-food program, Saddam was able to put the international community in the untenable situation of maintaining sanctions that were systematically starving the Iraqi people.[12] Bush had described the new world order as one that would be "freer from the threat of terror, stronger in the pursuit of justice, and more secure in the quest for peace."[13] The Persian Gulf War was waged to foster that vision. Yet those aspirations were belied by the effort to enforce Iraq's compliance with the postwar settlement terms imposed by the UN.

Bush envisioned a world order founded on collective security and the rule of law, a stable international environment that would allow democracy and free markets to spread to places they were once previously denied. In this new world, the United States would help forge consensus, facilitate collaboration, and support international responses to interstate aggression. Reflecting the postwar optimism, Bush's August

1991 National Security Strategy declared, "In the Gulf we caught a glimmer of a better future—a new world community brought together by a growing consensus that force cannot be used to settle disputes and that when that consensus is broken, the world will respond." The UN, the document continues, played "the role dreamed of by its founders, with the world's leading nations orchestrating and sanctioning collective action against aggression."[14]

Although the Soviet Union was undergoing a fraught process of political and economic liberalization, Bush believed that Mikhail Gorbachev was an indispensable partner in this order building effort. Yet, the Gulf War drove a wedge between Bush and Gorbachev. Gorbachev went along with Bush in coercing Saddam to quit Kuwait, but his understanding of the new world order was incompatible with the use of force. To avoid a major regional war, the Soviet leader tried to construct off-ramps for Bush and Saddam to take, none of which were pursued. More fundamentally, American diplomacy conflicted with Gorbachev's own conception of international leadership. As the historian Sergey Radchenko describes, Gorbachev's "New Thinking" was premised on two big ideas: first, that global leadership meant that the Soviet Union would be seen and treated as a great power equal to the United States, and second that "greatness was in projecting new ideas, and in showing a good example to the world by doing things others would deem naïve, or even dangerous: ending the arms race and pulling back from quasi-imperialistic foreign ventures."[15] The American-led war against Iraq violated both principles of New Thinking. Not only did Gorbachev's influence over events wane with the passing of UN Security Council Resolution 678 in November 1990 but Bush's determination to bloody Iraq for its transgression was precisely the type of quasi-imperialist venture Gorbachev wanted to avoid. While the war itself did not permanently damage US-Soviet relations, it showed the limits of great power cooperation going forward.

Separately, Gorbachev's standing at home was increasingly in doubt.[16] His political and economic reforms proved incapable of rescuing the USSR from a death spiral caused by falling oil prices and the unwillingness of the Communist Party to fully reform the country's command economy. Not only was economic growth elusive but Gorbachev's plans to politically restructure the Soviet Union succumbed to nationalist pressures building in the country's constituent republics. A three-day coup was launched against Gorbachev in August 1991, arousing fears in Washington that the USSR would reverse the progress made in Soviet-American relations. Although Gorbachev survived the putsch, his days as the leader of the USSR were numbered. Boris Yeltsin, the populist former mayor of Moscow and newly elected president of the Russian Soviet Federative Republic, was distrusted by senior officials in Washington. The Baltic states declared their independence in September, and in early December Yeltsin, Ukrainian president Leonid Kravchuk, and Belarusian parliament chairman Stanislav Shushkevich declared the creation of the Commonwealth of Independent States. Gorbachev resigned on December 25 and on the thirty-first the USSR ceased to exist.[17] Weakened economically and militarily, the Russian Federation that emerged as the USSR's successor state lacked the influence in global affairs that the Soviet Union once wielded. Many American officials concluded the United States alone bore the burden of shaping an international system in transition.

The continuation of military operations against Iraq by the United States after the Gulf War, the unanticipated emergence of violent internal conflicts in countries around the world, the cruelties Saddam imposed on his own people as he defied the UN, and the demise of the Soviet Union together exposed critical weaknesses of the New World Order grand strategy. Bush's confidence in his own grand strategy waned in the face of these challenges. As instability around the world grew (including a coup in Haiti, starvation and civil war in Somalia, and the secessionist wars in Yugoslavia), Bush eventually renounced the notion that an overarching set of principles guided America's foreign relations. Completely reversing his beliefs from spring 1989 through the Persian Gulf War, Bush remarked at the end of his presidency, "There can be no single or simple set of guidelines for foreign policy."[18]

The president's disillusionment with his strategy had significant bureaucratic implications. Bush was the chief architect of, and advocate for, the new world order. Brent Scowcroft, an exemplary national security adviser who served the president well by consistently providing him with a wealth of information and by running an effective decision-making process, was philosophically a realist who was more skeptical of the idealistic elements of Bush's approach. Baker's leadership at the State Department was also successful, but his strengths were in bargaining and diplomatic deal-making; he lacked Bush's strategic vision.

The new world order concept was never embraced in the Department of Defense. Cheney and his team were advocates of American primacy, an approach that sought to place US power at the forefront of American grand strategy. From 1989 to mid-1991, there was little that Cheney and his advisers could do to stymie or change Bush's strategic approach. Bush believed his grand strategy was succeeding and Scowcroft's management of the foreign policy process ensured that Bush's strategic beliefs, and no one else's, guided US statecraft. Bureaucratic space for an alternative to the New World Order grand strategy opened only when Bush lost faith in the approach in mid- to late 1991.

On March 8, 1992, the *New York Times* ran a front-page story detailing a secret strategy document circulating at the highest levels of the Department of Defense that envisioned an expansive and assertive role for the United States in the post–Cold War era. "With its focus on this concept of benevolent domination by one power," the *Times* report read, "the Pentagon document articulates the clearest rejection to date of collective internationalism, the strategy that emerged from World War II when the five victorious powers sought to form a United Nations that could mediate disputes and police outbreaks of violence." The objective of American grand strategy in this new international system should be "to prevent any hostile power from dominating a region whose resources would, under consolidated control, be sufficient to generate global power." Chief among the drafters' concerns were "advanced industrial nations" who would need to be dissuaded "from challenging our leadership or seeking to overturn the established political and economic order."[19]

Notwithstanding its anodyne title, Defense Planning Guidance, FY 1994–1999 (DPG), the leaked document generated enough controversy that the Bush administration distanced itself from the ideas embodied in it. The principal source of the controversy was the document's skepticism of the intentions of America's putative allies (both Japan and Germany were advanced industrial nations) and its apparent rejection of multilateralism through the United Nations.²⁰ While the White House refused to embrace the DPG, policymakers in the Pentagon set out to refine it. To temper criticisms aimed at the document's slighting of the UN, for example, the revised document, the Regional Defense Strategy, was peppered with salutary nods to multilateralism. Nevertheless, the Regional Defense Strategy's clear objective remained that of dissuasion: the United States should maintain military overmatch to such an extent that no other state would even contemplate competing with the lone superpower.²¹

The Defense Planning Guidance was an agenda-setting move by the DOD, an attempt to replace the new world order vision for one of American primacy.²² While some of the DOD's ideas made their way into Bush's 1993 National Security Strategy, the DPG would ultimately not be codified as America's grand strategy during Bush's single term in office.²³ Had Bush won a second term, there would likely have been a bruising battle waged over the new world order's successor, given that the DOD's alternative was viewed by Scowcroft as "arrogant," a conclusion that Bush likely shared.²⁴ Nevertheless, the emergence of the DPG in March 1992 had the effect of altering the debate over America's role in the world. The limitations of the New World Order grand strategy contrasted with an attractive primacist strategic logic that gradually produced a consensus in favor of a more muscular and less fettered approach to American statecraft.²⁵

The Gulf War's outcomes, both in terms of the magnitude of the coalition's military victory and lengths to which the United States needed to go to contain Saddam's belligerence after the war, led policymakers to the view that "the United States' status as the world's sole superpower was politically and military possible—and indeed necessary—to defend U.S. national interests in the post-Cold War world."²⁶ The war showed that America's technological superiority could easily overmatch any regional power, and further, that the United States had to preserve and extend its forward military presence to deter threats to its interests around the world. Bush never sought American hegemony outright. His vision of world order necessitated American leadership, but that leadership was intended to facilitate institutionalized cooperation among the great powers through the United Nations system. The Persian Gulf War convinced many officials in Washington that American national security could be fostered without having to accept the institutional restraints Bush thought were necessary. The price of hegemony after the Gulf War looked more like a bargain.

And yet, elements of the New World Order grand strategy created opportunities for subsequent American presidents. The central role of the UN in Bush's order-building effort, for example, imbued the institution with new life at a critical moment. Soon after the Gulf War, the UN showed itself willing to take on the challenges of civil wars, ethnic conflicts, and gross violations of human rights. In 1993 Bill Clinton's foreign policy team introduced a doctrine of "Assertive Multilateralism," an approach to humanitarian interventions that used the UN as a forum for exercising American leadership in a way that enhanced legitimacy and kept a lid on resource expenditures.[27] Clinton's grand strategy did incorporate the DPG's goal preventing the rise of a peer competitor, but primacy was not its sole objective. Rather, Clinton's approach blended primacy and multilateralism to advance American security, promote democracy, and foster an open international economic system.[28] Throughout the 1990s American statecraft reflected the lessons of the new world order experience—both its successes and its failures.

The United States went to war in January 1991 for a host of discrete reasons. We can pick through the documentary record and find statements from Bush administration officials emphasizing the threat Saddam would pose to international oil markets if his aggression went unchallenged, his ability to upend the balance of power in the Gulf region, and his approximation to Adolf Hitler. Each of these factors mattered in Bush's calculations for war, but to understand how, our analysis must home in on American grand strategy.

The New World Order grand strategy emerged from the set of strategic beliefs Bush formed before assuming the presidency. These ideas pertained to America's role in the world, the nature of the threats to the country and its interests abroad, the relative utility of the instruments of statecraft, and the value of information diversity in crafting policy. Bush was a committed internationalist who believed that, when possible, cooperation among states was the surest route to security and prosperity. Working together with others—preferably in the context of the UN system—often forged common interests and enabled countries to manage international crises more effectively. As relations with the Soviet Union improved in the second half of the 1980s, Bush saw an opportunity to promote US values—democracy and free markets—behind the Iron Curtain. But Bush was no ideological crusader. He recognized that although international trends were going America's way, they could be easily reversed. As such, he acted cautiously to foster these developments. Bush believed that uncertainty, instability, and volatility were endemic threats in the system, the management of which required steady American leadership. Bush's conception of power was holistic and sophisticated. US influence did not rest solely on its military strength, or the size of its national economy, or on the various diplomatic instruments available to the president. Strong international leadership meant marshalling all these resources and shrewdly discerning which commitments were imperative and which were peripheral. Because the international system was both complex and dynamic, Bush believed effective statecraft required leaders to avail themselves of information from a diversity of sources. Together, these ideas constituted Bush's "ecological world view," the ideas that would produce his New World Order grand strategy and guide his administration's actions during his four years in the White House.[29]

Translating Bush's strategic beliefs into a grand strategy was neither automatic nor easy. Although Secretary of State James Baker shared many of Bush's beliefs, Secretary of Defense Dick Cheney did not. The bureaucracies that these two oversaw, moreover, were populated with officials who shared their respective principal's ideas and who would work tirelessly to promote their department's prerogatives. To ensure that US grand strategy wasn't captured by others' preferences or fell victim to bureaucratic wrangling, Bush and his national security adviser Brent Scowcroft designed a system of strategic decision-making that empowered the president and effectively leveraged the talents and capacities across the national security bureaucracy. Bush's foreign policy process afforded him a wealth of quality information from multiple organizational sources, fostered timely bureaucratic collaboration, and ultimately enabled his beliefs to guide American statecraft. The New

World Order grand strategy was the product of Bush's beliefs and this decision-making system.

From spring 1989 to summer 1990, Bush's New World Order grand strategy aimed to end the Cold War in Europe. Bush sought to promote economic and political liberalization in the states of the Eastern Bloc, end the division of Europe by incorporating a unified Germany into a transformed NATO, and move beyond containment by working to incorporate the Soviet Union into the Western economic and security order. To achieve these objectives Bush systematically and skillfully employed all the tools of statecraft. Threats to these objectives, Bush assessed, were amorphous, but nevertheless real: the uncertainty, instability, and potential volatility inherent to an international system undergoing profound change. To mitigate those threats, Bush refused to make demands or act in ways that threatened Gorbachev's position at home. More broadly, he sought to cordon off Europe from sources of instability abroad, most notably from China. Iraq's invasion of Kuwait was different, however. Saddam posed a threat to the emerging order that had to be addressed directly. Bush's New World Order grand strategy proved highly effective in managing the Cold War's end.

The Gulf War was fought to achieve specific grand strategic objectives, most importantly to situate the UN collective security function at the heart of the new world order. To alter the order of the system so dramatically after decades of cold war, and to make that reorientation durable, the waging of the Gulf War had to be guided by certain principles. First, the political coalition confronting Iraq had to be as broad as possible and had to be sanctioned by the UN Security Council. Second, Arab partners had to contribute forces to the military coalition to ensure that the war and its aftermath were viewed legitimately in the region and beyond. Third, Saddam's forces had to be sufficiently destroyed to satisfy Arab states' security concerns. At the same time, Iraq had to retain enough power so that it could serve as a regional counterweight to Iran. This balance of power logic was subservient to the larger institutional and normative objectives of Bush's New World Order grand strategy. Collective security through the UN had to show that it could produce stable and broadly satisfactory outcomes with minimal intervention by outside powers.

The origins and prosecution of the Gulf War were heavily influenced by Bush's broader strategic vision for global order. But the administration was unable to convert the coalition's battlefield successes into grand strategic gains. Bush's decision to end the war before the Iraqi army south of the Euphrates River was fully destroyed allowed Saddam to suppress challenges to his regime. The ad hoc nature of the postwar settlement, moreover, limited America's ability to respond to Saddam's defiance in the ensuing months and years. At the same time, the war brought home the reality of the United States' preponderance of power. The United States didn't need to make a bid for hegemony. After the Soviet Union collapsed, America stood astride the world the way no other state in history had. To many American policymakers, security and prosperity didn't require the United States to accept the restrictions on its autonomy that collective security demands. The Gulf War did usher in a new world order, but it wasn't the one Bush had anticipated.

NOTES

INTRODUCTION

1. Lawrence G. Potter and Gary G. Sick, "Introduction," in *Iran, Iraq, and the Legacies of War*, ed. Lawrence G. Potter and Gary G. Sick (New York: Palgrave MacMillan, 2004), 8; Pierre Razoux, *The Iran-Iraq War*, trans. Nicholas Elliott (Cambridge, MA: Belknap Press, 2015).

2. Lawrence Freedman, *A Choice of Enemies: America Confronts the Middle East* (New York: PublicAffairs, 2008), 219.

3. Kevin M. Woods, David D. Palkki, and Mark E. Strout, eds., *The Saddam Tapes: The Inner Workings of a Tyrant's Regime, 1978-2001* (New York: Cambridge University Press, 2011), 167.

4. Shibley Telhami, "The Arab Dimension of Saddam Hussein's Calculations: What We Have Learned from Iraqi Records," in *Into the Desert: Reflections on the Gulf War*, ed. Jeffrey A. Engel (New York: Oxford University Press, 2013), 148-168.

5. Brent Scowcroft interview 2, August 10-11, 2000, George H. W. Bush Oral History Project, Miller Center, University of Virginia (hereafter BOHP).

6. James A. Baker III with Thomas M. DeFrank, *The Politics of Diplomacy: Revolution, War, and Peace, 1989-1992* (New York: Putnam, 1995), 277-278.

7. Michael R. Gordon and General Bernard E. Trainor, *The General's War: The Inside Story of the Conflict in the Gulf* (Boston: Little, Brown, 1995), ix.

8. Daryl G. Press, "The Myth of Air Power in the Persian Gulf War and the Future of Warfare," *International Security* 26, no. 2 (Fall 2001): 31.

9. Stephen Biddle, *Military Power: Explaining Victory and Defeat in Modern Battle* (Princeton, NJ: Princeton University Press, 2004), 135-149.

10. Rick Atkinson, *Crusade: The Untold Story of the Persian Gulf War* (New York: Houghton Mifflin, 1993), 248-253.

11. Brig. Gen. Robert H. Scales Jr., *Certain Victory: The U.S. Army in the Gulf War* (Washington, DC: Brassey's, 1994), 128-133.

12. Michael O'Hanlon, "Estimating Casualties in a War to Overthrow Saddam," *Orbis* 47, no. 1 (Winter 2003): 29.

13. Spencer D. Bakich, *Success and Failure in Limited War: Information and Strategy in the Korean, Vietnam, Persian Gulf, and Iraq Wars* (Chicago: University of Chicago Press, 2014).

14. John Mueller, *Policy and Opinion in the Gulf War* (Chicago: University of Chicago Press, 1994), 49-58.

15. William C. Martel, *Victory in War: Foundations of Modern Strategy* (New York: Cambridge University Press, 2011), 154-158.

16. Joshua Rovner, "Delusion of Defeat: The United States and Iraq, 1990-1998," *Journal of Strategic Studies* 17, no. 4 (June 2014): 485-486.

17. Russell A. Burgos, "Origins of Regime Change: 'Ideapolitik' on the Long Road to Baghdad, 1993-2000," *Security Studies* 17, no. 2 (May 2008): 237-255.

CHAPTER 1. GEORGE BUSH: PRESIDENT AND STRATEGIST

1. Jeffrey A. Engel, *The China Diary of George H. W. Bush: The Making of a Global President* (Princeton, NJ: Princeton University Press, 2008), 408.
2. Quoted in Engel, *China Diary*, 411.
3. Jeffrey A. Engel, *When the World Seemed New: George H. W. Bush and the End of the Cold War* (New York: Houghton Mifflin Harcourt, 2017), 38–39.
4. Hugh Heclo, "George Bush and American Conservatism," in *41: Inside the Presidency of George H. W. Bush*, ed. Michael Nelson and Barbara Perry (Ithaca, NY: Cornell University Press, 2014), 60.
5. Chase Untermeyer, "The Accidental Diplomat: Staffing Foreign Policy," in *Transforming Our World: President George H. W. Bush and American Foreign Policy*, ed. Andrew S. Natsios and Andrew H. Card Jr. (New York: Rowman & Littlefield, 2020), 33.
6. George Bush diary entry Sunday, July 6, 1975, in Engel, *China Diary*, 353.
7. Engel, *China Diary*, 434–442.
8. Engel, *China Diary*, 445.
9. George Bush diary entry November 15, 1974, in Engel, *China Diary*, 75.
10. George Bush diary entry November 26, 1974, in Engel, *China Diary*, 97.
11. George Bush diary entry November 5, 1974, in Engel, *China Diary*, 57.
12. Engle, *China Diary*, 430
13. George Bush diary entry April 8, 1975, in Engel, *China Diary*, 243.
14. James Mann, *Rise of the Vulcans: The History of Bush's War Cabinet* (New York: Viking, 2004), 74–75.
15. Joshua Rovner, *Fixing the Facts: National Security and the Politics of Intelligence* (Ithaca, NY: Cornell University Press, 2011), 125.
16. Willard C. Matthias, *America's Strategic Blunders: Intelligence Analysis and National Security Policy, 1946–1991* (University Park: Penn State Press, 2001), 304–311.
17. Jon Meacham, *Destiny and Power: The American Odyssey of George Herbert Walker Bush* (New York: Random House, 2015), 201–202.
18. Untermeyer, "Accidental Diplomat," 33.
19. Tim Weiner, *Legacy of Ashes: The History of the CIA* (New York: Doubleday, 2007), 352.
20. Meacham, *Destiny and Power*, 262–265.
21. Robert M. Gates, *Duty: Memoirs of a Secretary at War* (New York: Knopf, 2014), 282.
22. Quoted in Ivo H. Daalder and I. M. Destler, *In the Shadow of the Oval Office: Profiles of the National Security Advisers and the Presidents They Served—From JFK to George W. Bush* (New York: Simon and Schuster, 2009), 133.
23. David Rothkopf, *Running the World: The Inside Story of the National Security Council and the Architects of American Power* (New York: PublicAffairs, 2005), 216.
24. Robert M. Gates, *From the Shadows: The Ultimate Insider's Story of Five*

Presidents and How They Won the Cold War (New York: Simon and Schuster, 1996), 283.

25. Rothkopf, *Running the World*, 218.

26. Meacham, *Destiny and Power*, 285-286.

27. Simon Miles, *Engaging the Evil Empire: Washington, Moscow, and the Beginning of the End of the Cold War* (Ithaca, NY: Cornell University Press, 2020), 60-61, 82-83, 112.

28. George H. W. Bush, *All the Best: My Life in Letters and Other Writings* (New York: Scribner, 2013), 321.

29. William Inboden, *The Peacemaker: Ronald Reagan, the Cold War, and the World on the Brink* (New York: Dutton, 2022), 328-332.

30. Derek Chollet, *The Middle Way: How Three Presidents Shaped America's Role in the World* (New York: Oxford University Press, 2021), 35-41.

31. Richard Haass, "The Compassionate Realist: An Overview," in Natsios and Card, *Transforming Our World*, 17; Henry Kissinger, *World Order* (New York: Penguin Press, 2014), 314-315.

32. A quantitative assessment of Bush's operational code shows a preference for high levels of cooperation over goals (strategic), but moderate levels of cooperation on tactics. Stephen G. Walker, Mark Schaefer, and Michael D. Young, "Presidential Operational Codes and Foreign Policy Conflicts in the Post-Cold War World," *Journal of Conflict Resolution* 43, no. 5 (October 1999): 617-619.

33. Engel, *When the World Seemed New*, 22, 73.

34. Carla A. Hills, "President George H. W. Bush's Historic Contributions to Open Trade," in Natsios and Card, *Transforming Our World*, 159-162.

35. James A. Baker III, "Ten Foreign Policy Maxims of a Great President," in Natsios and Card, *Transforming Our World*, 13.

36. Chollet, *Middle Way*, 21-23.

37. Robert A. Strong, *Character and Consequence: Foreign Policy Decisions of George H. W. Bush* (Lanham, MD: Lexington Books, 2020), 143-146.

38. Engel, *When the World Seemed New*, 6.

39. Peter Baker and Susan Glasser, *The Man Who Ran Washington: The Life and Times of James A. Baker III* (New York: Doubleday, 2020), 374.

40. Quoted in Bartholomew Sparrow, *The Strategist: Brent Scowcroft and the Call of National Security* (New York: PublicAffairs, 2015), 271-272.

41. Haass, "The Compassionate Realist," in *Transforming Our World*, 19.

42. Baker and Glasser, *Man Who Ran Washington*, 331.

43. Brent Scowcroft interview 1, November 12-13, 1999, BOHP.

44. Philip Zelikow, "Brent Scowcroft and American Military Intervention," *War on the Rocks*, August 2, 2020.

45. Robert A. Strong, "Character and Consequence: The John Tower Confirmation Battle," in Nelson and Perry, *41*, 122-123.

46. Dick Cheney with Liz Cheney, *In My Time: A Personal and Political Memoir* (New York: Threshold Editions, 2011), 205.

47. Mann, *Rise of the Vulcans*, 200-201.

48. James Mann, *The Great Rift: Dick Cheney, Colin Powell, and the Broken Friendship That Defined an Era* (New York: Henry Holt, 2020), 87–97.

49. Engel, *When the World Seemed New*, 128–129.

50. Mann, *Great Rift*, 92–96; Cheney, *In My Time*, 171.

51. Karl F. Inderfurth and Loch K. Johnson, "National Security Advisers: Roles," in *Fateful Decisions: Inside the National Security Council*, ed. Karl F. Inderfurth and Loch K. Johnson (New York: Oxford University Press, 2004), 131–140.

52. Remarks by Philip Zelikow in "Oral History Roundtables: The Bush Administration National Security Council," in *The National Security Council Project*, ed. Ivo H. Daalder and I. M. Destler (Washington, DC: Brookings Institution, 1999), 5.

53. Sparrow, *Strategist*, 555.

54. Sparrow, *Strategist*, 555.

55. Jane Holl Lute, "Remaking the National Security Council: Bush, Scowcroft, and Institutional Reform," in Natsios and Card, *Transforming Our World*, 43.

56. John Gans, *White House Warriors: How the National Security Council Transformed the American Way of War* (New York: Liverlight, 2019), 88.

57. George Bush and Brent Scowcroft, *A World Transformed* (New York: Knopf, 1998), 31.

58. National Security Directive 1, "Organization of the National Security Council System," January 30,1989, George H. W. Presidential Library & Museum, available at https://bush41library.tamu.edu/files/nsd/nsd1.pdf.

59. Supplement to National Security Directive 1 (Crisis Management), October 25, 1989, George H. W. Presidential Library & Museum, available at https://bush41library.tamu.edu/files/nsd/nsd1a.pdf.

60. Mark Wilcox, "The National Security Council Deputies Committee: Engine of the Policy Process," *Interagency Journal* 5, no. 1 (Winter 2014): 23–24.

61. Rothkopf, *Running the World*, 267.

62. Robert M. Gates interview, July 23–24, 2000, BOHP.

63. Remarks by Philip Zelikow in "Oral History Roundtables," 32.

64. Scowcroft interview 1, BOHP.

65. Spencer D. Bakich, *Success and Failure in Limited War: Information and Strategy in the Korean, Vietnam, Persian Gulf, and Iraq Wars* (Chicago: University of Chicago Press, 2014), 179–182.

66. Gates interview, BOHP.

CHAPTER 2. THE NEW WORLD ORDER GRAND STRATEGY, 1989–1990

1. Jeffrey A. Engel, "1989: An Introduction to an International History," in *The Fall of the Berlin Wall: The Revolutionary Legacy of 1989*, ed. Jeffrey A. Engel (New York: Oxford University Press, 2009), 27–28.

2. Quoted in Melvyn P. Leffler, *For the Soul of Mankind: The United States, the Soviet Union, and the Cold War* (New York: Hill and Wang, 2007), 421–424.

3. George Bush and Brent Scowcroft, *A World Transformed* (New York: Knopf, 1998), 8–9.

4. Quoted in Philip Zelikow and Condoleezza Rice, *Germany Unified and Europe Transformed: A Study in Statecraft* (Cambridge, MA: Harvard University Press, 1997), 24.

5. Michael Cox and Steven Hurst, "'His Finest Hour?' George Bush and the Diplomacy of German Unification," *Diplomacy and Statecraft* 13, no. 4 (December 2002): 133.

6. Zelikow and Rice, *Germany Unified and Europe Transformed*, 31; Jeffrey A. Engel, *When the World Seemed New: George H. W. Bush and the End of the Cold War* (New York: Houghton Mifflin Harcourt, 2017), 73.

7. Leffler, *For the Soul of Mankind*, 438.

8. Bush and Scowcroft, *World Transformed*, 240–241.

9. Mary Elise Sarotte, *1989: The Struggle to Create Post–Cold War Europe* (Princeton, NJ: Princeton University Press, 2009), 65–66.

10. George H. W. Bush, "The President's News Conference in Helena, Montana," September 18, 1989, George H. W. Bush Presidential Library & Museum, https://bush41library.tamu.edu/archives/public-papers/929.

11. Mark L. Haas, "The United States and the End of the Cold War: Reactions to Shifts in Soviet Power, Policies, or Domestic Politics?" *International Organization* 61, no. 1 (January 2007): 171.

12. George H. W. Bush, "Remarks to Citizens in Hamtramck, Michigan," April 17, 1989, George H. W. Bush Presidential Library & Museum, https://bush41library.tamu.edu/archives/public-papers/326; Bush and Scowcroft, *World Transformed*, 48–49.

13. Brent Scowcroft interview 1, November 12–13, 1999, BOHP.

14. M. E. Sarotte, *Not One Inch: American, Russia, and the Making of the Post–Cold War Stalemate* (New Haven: Yale University Press, 2021), 29.

15. Kristina Spohr, *Post Wall, Post Square: How Bush, Gorbachev, Kohl, and Deng Shaped the World after 1989* (New Haven: Yale University Press, 2020), 92–95.

16. George H. W. Bush, "Remarks to the Citizens in Mainz, Federal Republic of Germany," May 31, 1989, George H. W. Bush Presidential Library & Museum, https://bush41library.tamu.edu/archives/public-papers/476.

17. Peter Baker and Susan Glasser, *The Man Who Ran Washington: The Life and Times of James A. Baker III* (New York: Doubleday, 2020), 363.

18. Zelikow and Rice, *Germany United and Europe Transformed*, 131–134.

19. Melvyn P. Leffler, "Dreams of Freedom, Temptations of Power," in Engel, *Fall of the Berlin Wall*, 140.

20. National Security Directive 23 (NSD-23), "United States Relations with the Soviet Union," September 22, 1989, George H. W. Bush Presidential Library & Museum, https://bush41library.tamu.edu/files/nsd/nsd23.pdf.

21. George H. W. Bush, "Commencement Address at Texas A&M University," May 12, 1989, University of Virginia, Miller Center, https://millercenter.org/the

-presidency/presidential-speeches/may-12-1989-commencement-address-texas-am-university.

22. NSD-23.
23. NSD-23.
24. George H. W. Bush, "Remarks at the United States Coast Guard Academy Commencement Ceremony in New London, Connecticut," May 24, 1989, https://bush41library.tamu.edu/archives/public-papers/448.
25. Spohr, *Post Wall, Post Square*, 42.
26. James A. Baker III, "A New Europe, A New Atlanticism: Architecture for a New Era," *Current Policy* no. 1233 (Washington, DC: United States Department of State, December 12, 1989).
27. Bush and Scowcroft, *World Transformed*, 234, 240; Engel, *When the World Seemed New*, 340–341.
28. Officials in the Bush administration understood that Soviet conventional force reductions had implications both for the strategic military balance and for democratization in Europe. Scowcroft interview 1, BOHP.
29. Hal Brands, *Making the Unipolar Moment: U.S. Foreign Policy and the Rise of the Post–Cold War Order* (Ithaca, NY: Cornell University Press, 2016), 274–276.
30. Robert B. Zoellick, "Bush 41 and Gorbachev," *Diplomatic History* 42, no. 4 (September 2018): 561–562.
31. George H. W. Bush, *All the Best: My Life in Letters and Other Writings* (New York: Scribner, 2013), 460–461.
32. Horst Teltschik, "President George H. W. Bush: A Stroke of Luck for Germany," in *Transforming Our World: President George H. W. Bush and American Foreign Policy*, ed. Andrew S. Natsios and Andrew H. Card (New York: Rowman & Littlefield, 2020), 84.
33. Sarotte, *Not One Inch*, 38.
34. George H. W. Bush, "Outline of Remarks at the North Atlantic Treaty Organization Headquarters in Brussels," December 4, 1989, George H. W. Bush Presidential Library & Museum, https://bush41library.tamu.edu/archives/public-papers/1297.
35. Philip Zelikow and Condoleezza Rice, *To Build a Better World: Choices to End the Cold War and Create a Global Commonwealth* (New York: Twelve, 2019), 205.
36. William J. Burns, *The Back Channel: A Memoir of American Diplomacy and the Case for Its Renewal* (New York: Random House, 2019), 54–55.
37. Cox and Hurst, "'His Finest Hour?'" 136–138.
38. Bartholomew Sparrow, *The Strategist: Brent Scowcroft and the Call of National Security* (New York: PublicAffairs, 2015), 373.
39. "The Basic Law of the FRG, May 23, 1949," Université du Luxembourg, Luxembourg Centre for Contemporary and Digital History, https://www.cvce.eu/content/publication/1999/1/1/7fa618bb-604e-4980-b667-76bf0cd0dd9b/publishable_en.pdf.
40. Zelikow and Rice, *German Unified and Europe Transformed*, 198–217.

41. Sarotte, *Not One Inch*, 73-74.

42. James A. Baker III with Thomas M. DeFrank, *The Politics of Diplomacy: Revolution, War, and Peace, 1989-1992* (New York: Putnam, 1995), 212.

43. James Graham Wilson, *The Triumph of Improvisation: Gorbachev's Adaptation, Reagan's Engagement, and the End of the Cold War* (Ithaca, NY: Cornell University Press, 2014), 175.

44. Michael R. Beschloss and Strobe Talbott, *At the Highest Levels: The Inside Story of the End of the Cold War* (Boston: Little, Brown, 1993), 74-80.

45. Quoted in Gordon S. Barrass, *The Great Cold War: A Journey through the Hall of Mirrors* (Stanford, CA: Stanford University Press, 2009), 359.

46. Engel, *When the World Seemed New*, 297-303.

47. Zelikow and Rice, *Germany Unified and Europe Transformed*, 127-129.

48. Baker noted that at the Malta summit, the Americans "came to the conclusion that these guys were genuine reformers, that we should work with them, that we could work with them, and that we hoped that they would succeed in the perestroika and glasnost." James A. Baker III interview, March 17, 2011, BOHP.

49. Sparrow, *Strategist*, 372-374.

50. Bush and Scowcroft, *World Transformed*, 282.

51. Zelikow and Rice, *Germany Unified and Europe Transformed*, 279. See also Zelikow and Rice, *To Build a Better World*, 275-281. In their meeting, Gorbachev was the first to raise the issue of self-determination, an opening that allowed Bush "to nail him on Helsinki." Spohr, *Post Wall, Post Square*, 234.

52. Zoellick, "Bush 41 and Gorbachev," 562.

53. Quoted in Sarotte, *Not One Inch*, 55; Zoellick, "Bush 41 and Gorbachev," 562. For a sampling of this debate, see Joshua R. Itzkowitz Shifrinson, "Deal or No Deal? The End of the Cold War and the U.S. Offer to Limit NATO Expansion," *International Security* 40, no. 4 (Spring 2016): 7-44; Kristina Spohr, "Precluded or Precedent-Setting? The 'NATO Enlargement Question' in the Triangular Bonn-Washington-Moscow Diplomacy of 1990-1991," *Journal of Cold War Studies* 14, no. 4 (Fall 2012): 18-32; and Zelikow and Rice, *To Build a Better World*, 477n50.

54. Sarotte, *Not One Inch*, 66.

55. "Excerpt from Evgeny Primakov Memoir on NATO Expansion," January 1, 1996, National Security Archive, https://nsarchive.gwu.edu/document/16394-document-22-excerpt-evgeny-primakov-memoir.

56. Engel, *When the World Seemed New*, 350.

57. Sarotte, *Not One Inch*, 73, 102.

58. George H. W. Bush, "Remarks at the Oklahoma State University Commencement Ceremony in Stillwater," May 4, 1990, in George H. W. Bush Presidential Library & Museum, https://bush41library.tamu.edu/archives/public-papers/1853.

59. Raymond L. Garthoff, *Détente and Confrontation: American-Soviet Relations from Nixon to Reagan* (Washington, DC: Brookings Institution Press, 1994), 527-532.

60. David Remnik, "Gorbachev Pledges to Use Powers for Economy, New Security Plan," *Washington Post*, March 16, 1990.
61. Spohr, *Post Wall, Post Square*, 316.
62. Bush and Scowcroft, *World Transformed*, 268-269, 292-296.
63. Zelikow and Rice, *To Build a Better World*, 301.
64. R. W. Apple Jr., "East and West Sign Pact to Shed Arms in Europe," *New York Times*, November 20, 1990.
65. Christian Peterson, "H-Diplo FRUS Review of James Graham Wilson ed. *Foreign Relations of the United States, 1981-1988*, Volume VI, Soviet Union, October 1986-1989. Washington, D.C.: United States Government Publishing Office (GPO), 2016," *H-Diplo* (June 2019): 10-11.
66. German unification occurred on October 3, 1990.
67. Scowcroft interview 1, BOHP.
68. Jeffrey A. Engel, "A Better World . . . but Don't Get Carried Away: The Foreign Policy of George H. W. Bush Twenty Years On," *Diplomatic History* 34, no. 1 (January 2010): 32.
69. Stephen G. Walker et al., "Presidential Operational Codes and Foreign Policy Conflicts in the Post-Cold War World," *Journal of Conflict Resolution* 43, no. 5 (October 1999): 617-618.
70. Robert A. Strong, *Character and Consequence: Foreign Policy Decisions of George H. W. Bush* (Lanham, MD: Lexington Books, 2019), 119.
71. Spohr, *Post Wall, Post Square*, 28-29.
72. John Lewis Gaddis, *Strategies of Containment: A Critical Appraisal of American National Security Policy during the Cold War* (New York: Oxford University Press, 2005), 280.
73. Engel, *When the World Seemed New*, 105-106.
74. Robert G. Sutter, *U.S. Policy toward China: An Introduction to the Role of Interest Groups* (Lanham, MD: Rowman and Littlefield, 1998), 29-30.
75. David Rothkopf, *Running the World: The Inside Story of the National Security Council and the Architects of American Power* (New York: PublicAffairs, 2005), 290-291.
76. Engel, *When the World Seemed New*, 180, 194-195.
77. Michael J. Green, *By More Than Providence: Grand Strategy and American Power in the Asia Pacific Since 1783* (New York: Columbia University Press, 2017), 432, 435.
78. Scowcroft interview 1, BOHP.
79. Baker interview, BOHP.
80. Baker, *Politics of Diplomacy*, 116.
81. Baker and Glasser, *Man Who Ran Washington*, 332-335.
82. George H. W. Bush, "Statement on the Bipartisan Accord on Central America," March 24, 1989, American Presidency Project, https://www.presidency.ucsb.edu/documents/statement-the-bipartisan-accord-central-america.
83. William C. Martel, *Victory in War: Foundations of Modern Strategy*, rev. ed. (New York: Cambridge University Press, 2011), 225.

84. Dick Cheney with Liz Cheney, *In My Time: A Personal and Political Memoir* (New York: Threshold Editions, 2011), 166–167.
85. Peter Baker and Susan Glasser, "James Baker's 7 Rules for Running Washington," *Politico*, September 28, 2020; Beschloss and Talbott, *At the Highest Levels*, 55.
86. Zelikow and Rice, *To Build a Better World*, 138.
87. Scowcroft interview 1, BOHP.
88. Brent Scowcroft interview 2, August 10–11, 2000, BOHP.

CHAPTER 3. OPERATION DESERT SHIELD AND THE DECISION FOR WAR

1. Lawrence Freedman and Efraim Karsh, *The Gulf Conflict: Diplomacy and War in the New World Order* (Princeton, NJ: Princeton University Press, 1993), 50–55.
2. Garry R. Hess, *Presidential Decisions for War: Korea, Vietnam, the Persian Gulf, and Iraq*, 2nd ed. (Baltimore: Johns Hopkins University Press, 2009), 159.
3. Hess, *Presidential Decisions for War*, 160–161.
4. Bush telcon with King Hussein, July 31, 1990, George H. W. Bush Presidential Library & Museum, https://bush41library.tamu.edu/files/memcons-telcons/1990-07-31--Hussein%20I.pdf.
5. Christian Alfonsi, *Circle in the Sand: Why We Went Back to Iraq* (New York: Doubleday, 2006), 25–49.
6. Dick Cheney with Liz Cheney, *In My Time: A Personal and Political Memoir* (New York: Threshold Editions, 2011), 183.
7. NSC/DC Meetings—George H.W. Bush Administration (1989–1993), George H. W. Bush Presidential Library & Museum, https://bush41library.tamu.edu/files/nsc_and_dc_meetings_1989-1992-declassified.pdf.
8. Bob Woodward, *The Commanders* (New York: Touchstone, 1991), 223–224.
9. US News & World Report, *Triumph without Victory: The Unreported History of the Persian Gulf War* (New York: Times Books, 1992), 36–39.
10. George Bush and Brent Scowcroft, *A World Transformed* (New York: Knopf, 1998), 317–318.
11. Bartholomew Sparrow, *The Strategist: Brent Scowcroft and the Call of National Security* (New York: PublicAffairs, 2015), 387–388.
12. Richard N. Haass, *War of Necessity, War of Choice: A Memoir of Two Iraq Wars* (New York: Simon & Schuster, 2009), 62.
13. Eagleburger likely meant "post–Cold War system."
14. NSC Meeting on the Persian Gulf, August 3, 1990, Bush Library, NSC (Richard Haass Files), Working Files Iraq 2/8/90–12/90 (8 of 8).
15. Meeting of the National Security Council, August 4, 1990, National Security Archive, https://nsarchive.gwu.edu/document/24309-national-security-council-meeting-august-4-1990.
16. General H. Norman Schwarzkopf with Peter Petre, *It Doesn't Take a Hero* (New York: Bantam Books, 1992), 301.

17. Meeting of the National Security Council, August 4, 1990.

18. CENTCOM's OPLAN 90-1002 for the defense of Saudi Arabia was shared with Saudi ambassador to the United States Prince Bandar two days prior to Cheney's visit to Riyadh. Colin Powell with Joseph E. Persico, *My American Journey* (New York: Ballentine Books, 1995), 465.

19. Bush telcon with King Fahd, August 4, 1990, National Security Archive, https://nsarchive.gwu.edu/document/24310-bush-telcon-king-fahd-saudi-arabia-august-4-1990.

20. Bush and Scowcroft, *World Transformed*, 333.

21. National Security Directive-26, "U.S. Policy toward the Persian Gulf," October 2, 1989, p. 1, George H. W. Bush Presidential Library & Museum, https://bush41library.tamu.edu/files/nsd/nsd26.pdf.

22. Quoted in Melvyn P. Leffler, *Safeguarding Democratic Capitalism: U.S. Foreign Policy and National Security, 1920-2015* (Princeton, NJ: Princeton University Press, 2017), 258.

23. Jeffrey A. Engel, "The Gulf War at the End of the Cold War and Beyond," in *Into the Desert: Reflections on the Gulf War*, ed. Jeffrey A. Engel (New York: Oxford University Press, 2013), 36.

24. "No Vietnams," *Newsweek*, December 19, 1990; H. W. Brands, "Neither Munich nor Vietnam: The Gulf War of 1991," in *Power of the Past: History and Statecraft*, ed. Hal Brands and Jeremi Suri (Washington, DC: Brookings Institution Press, 2016), 73-74.

25. Quoted in Hal Brands, *Making the Unipolar Moment: U.S. Foreign Policy and the Rise of the Post-Cold War Order* (Ithaca, NY: Cornell University Press, 2016), 301.

26. James A. Baker III with Thomas M. DeFrank, *The Politics of Diplomacy: Revolution, War, and Peace, 1989-1992* (New York: Putnam, 1995), 14, 2.

27. Cheney, *In My Time*, 189-192.

28. Baker telcon with Shevardnadze, August 7, 1990, National Security Archive, https://nsarchive.gwu.edu/document/24312-secretary-state-james-baker-telcon-soviet-foreign-minister-eduard-shevardnadze.

29. Baker, *Politics of Diplomacy*, 282-283.

30. Bush and Scowcroft, *World Transformed*, 361-362, 364.

31. Anatoly Chernyaev, *My Six Years with Gorbachev*, ed. Robert English and Elizabeth Tucker (University Park: The Pennsylvania State University Press, 2000), 283-284.

32. Bush and Scowcroft, *World Transformed*, 365-366, 368.

33. National Security Directive 45, "U.S. Policy in Response to the Iraqi Invasion of Kuwait," August 20, 1990, George H. W. Bush Presidential Library & Museum, https://bush41library.tamu.edu/files/nsd/nsd45.pdf.

34. George H. W. Bush, "Address before a Joint Session of the Congress on the Persian Gulf Crisis and the Federal Budget Deficit," September 11, 1990, George H. W. Bush Presidential Library & Museum, https://bush41library.tamu.edu/archives/public-papers/2217.

35. Bush and Scowcroft, *World Transformed*, 400.

36. Bush, "Address before a Joint Session of the Congress."
37. George H. W. Bush, "Remarks to the Federal Assembly in Prague, Czechoslovakia," November 17, 1990, George H. W. Bush Presidential Library & Museum https://bush41library.tamu.edu/archives/public-papers/2461.
38. Henry Kissinger, *World Order* (New York: Penguin Press, 2014), 315.
39. Ashley Cox, *Wilsonian Approaches to American Conflicts: From the War of 1812 to the First Gulf War* (New York: Routledge: 2017), 116–135.
40. Tony Smith, *Why Wilson Matters: The Origin of American Liberal Internationalism and Its Crisis Today* (Princeton, NJ: Princeton University Press, 2017), 12.
41. Baker, *Politics of Diplomacy*, 277–278.
42. Philip Zelikow's remarks in Brent Scowcroft interview 2, August 10, 2000, BOHP.
43. Brent Scowcroft's remarks in Scowcroft interview 2, BOHP.
44. Freedman and Karsh, *Gulf Conflict*, 361.
45. Gorbachev memcon with Baker, September 13, 1990, National Security Archive, https://nsarchive.gwu.edu/document/24318-gorbachev-memcon-u-s-secretary-state-james-baker-moscow-september-13-1990.
46. Christopher Maynard, *Out of the Shadows: George H. W. Bush and the End of the Cold War* (College Station: Texas A&M University Press, 2008), 81–82.
47. Haass, *War of Necessity, War of Choice*, 71–72.
48. Alexander Thompson, *Channels of Power: The UN Security Council and U.S. Statecraft in Iraq* (Ithaca, NY: Cornell University Press, 2009), 71–73.
49. Mohamed Heikal, *Illusions of Triumph: An Arab View of the Gulf War* (New York: HarperCollins, 1992), 225–226.
50. Daniel Brumberg, "From Strategic Surprise to Strategic Gain: Egypt's Role in the Gulf Coalition," in *Friends in Need*, ed. Andrew Bennett, Joseph Lepgold, and Danny Unger (New York: St. Martin's, 1997), 97.
51. William Taubman, *Gorbachev: His Life and Times* (New York: Norton, 2017), 567.
52. Isabella Grunberg, "Still a Reluctant Ally? France's Participation in the Gulf War Coalition," in Bennett, Lepgold, and Unger, *Friends in Need*, 119.
53. Thomas Pickering interview, December 14, 2010, BOHP.
54. Thomas Pickering interview, July 21, 2006, Foreign Affairs Oral History Project, Association for Diplomatic Studies and Training (hereafter FAOHP).
55. Paul Kennedy, *The Parliament of Man: The Past, Present, and Future of the United Nations* (New York: Vintage 2006), 64.
56. Pickering interview, FAOHP.
57. Quoted in Jeffrey A. Engel, *When the World Seemed New: George H. W. Bush and the End of the Cold War* (New York: Houghton Mifflin Harcourt, 2017), 411.
58. Pickering spoke to Kimmitt, who then informed Baker. Pickering interview, FAOHP.
59. On institutional binding, see G. John Ikenberry, *After Victory: Institutions, Strategic Restraint, and the Rebuilding of Order after Major Wars* (Princeton, NJ: Princeton University Press, 2001), 40–42.

60. Chernyaev, *My Six Years with Gorbachev*, 284.

61. Michael Barnett, *Dialogues in Arab Politics*, 2nded. (New York: Columbia University Press, 1998), 216–218.

62. Patricia A. Weitsman, *Waging War: Alliances, Coalitions, and Institutions of Interstate Violence* (Stanford, CA: Stanford University Press, 2014), 66, 68–71.

63. Haass, *War of Necessity, War of Choice*, 79–80.

64. Schwarzkopf, *It Doesn't Take a Hero*, 345–346. Italics in original.

65. Woodward, *Commanders*, 41–42, 298–302.

66. David Jeremiah interview, November 15, 2010, BOHP.

67. Bush and Scowcroft, *World Transformed*, 374.

68. Quoted in Brands, "Neither Munich nor Vietnam," 79, 81.

69. Haass, *War of Necessity, War of Choice*, 94.

70. Alfonsi, *Circle in the Sand*, 121–125.

71. Powell, *My American Journey*, 480.

72. Powell, *My American Journey*, 487.

73. Robert M. Gates interview, July 23–24, 2000, BOHP. See also Robert A. Strong, *Character and Consequence: Foreign Policy Decisions of George H. W. Bush* (New York: Lexington Books, 2020), 112–114.

74. Kristina Spohr, *Post Wall, Post Square: How Bush, Gorbachev, Kohl, and Deng Shaped the World after 1989* (New Haven: Yale University Press, 2019), 356–357.

75. Gorbachev memcon with Mitterrand, October 29, 1990, National Security Archive, https://nsarchive.gwu.edu/document/24323-gorbachev-memcons-french-president-francois-mitterrand-prime-minister-rocard-and.

76. "Excerpts from Record of Conversation between M.S. Gorbachev and J. Baker," November 8, 1990, National Security Archive, https://nsarchive.gwu.edu/document/24324-gorbachev-memcon-u-s-secretary-state-james-baker-moscow-november-8-1990.

77. Cheney, for example, argued for an attack based on article 51 justification. Cheney, *In My Time*, 207.

78. Memorandum from Baker to Bush, "My Day in Moscow, November 8, 1990," November 8, 1990, National Security Archive, https://nsarchive.gwu.edu/document/24325-u-s-secretary-state-james-baker-president-bush-my-day-moscow-november-8-1990.

79. Gorbachev memcon with Bush, November 19, 1990, National Security Archive, https://nsarchive.gwu.edu/document/24326-bush-gorbachev-memcon-paris-november-19-1990.

80. Peter Baker and Susan Glasser, *The Man Who Ran Washington: The Life and Times of James A. Baker III* (New York: Doubleday, 2020), 412–413.

81. Thompson, *Channels of Power*, 46–47.

82. Bush, *All the Best*, 489.

83. Steve A. Yetiv, *Explaining Foreign Policy: U.S. Decision-Making in the Gulf Wars* (Baltimore: Johns Hopkins University Press, 2011), 164–166.

84. Thomas R. Pickering, "President George H. W. Bush and the United Nations," in *Transforming Our World: President George H. W. Bush and American For-*

eign Policy, ed. Andrew S. Natsios and Andre H. Card (New York: Rowman & Littlefield, 2020), 169.

85. Baker and Glasser, *The Man Who Ran Washington*, 414, 418-422.

CHAPTER 4. OPERATION DESERT STORM

1. General H. Norman Schwarzkopf with Peter Petre, *It Doesn't Take a Hero* (New York: Bantam Books, 1992), 313, 318-321.

2. *Conduct of the Persian Gulf War: Final Report to Congress* (Washington, DC: Department of Defense, 1992), 84.

3. Schwarzkopf, *It Doesn't Take a Hero*, 320-321.

4. An army corps consists of two to five divisions, between twenty and forty thousand soldiers, and is commanded by a three-star (lieutenant) general.

5. Schwarzkopf, *It Doesn't Take a Hero*, 356.

6. Colin Powell with Joseph E. Perisico, *My American Journey* (New York: Ballentine Books, 1995), 484.

7. Michael Gordon and General Bernard E. Trainor, *The Generals' War* (New York: Little, Brown, 1995), 133-139.

8. George Bush and Brent Scowcroft, *A World Transformed* (New York: Knopf, 1998), 381; on Cheney's concerns see Robert Coram, *Boyd: The Fighter Pilot Who Changed the Art of War* (Boston: Little, Brown, 2002), 423-424.

9. Rick Atkinson, *Crusade: The Untold Story of the Persian Gulf War* (New York: Houghton Mifflin, 1993), 110-111.

10. Dick Cheney with Liz Cheney, *In My Time: A Personal and Political Memoir* (New York: Threshold Editions, 2011), 200.

11. Henry S. Rowen, "Inchon in the Desert: My Rejected Plan," *National Interest* 40 (Summer 1995), 34-39.

12. David Jeremiah interview, November 15, 2010, BOHP.

13. Lawrence Freedman and Efraim Karsh, *The Gulf Conflict: Diplomacy and War in the New World Order, 1990-1991* (Princeton: Princeton University Press, 1993), 207-208.

14. Gordon and Trainor, *Generals' War*, 152.

15. Gordon and Trainor, *Generals' War*, 146-149.

16. Cheney, *In My Time*, 206.

17. Bob Woodward, *The Commanders* (New York: Touchstone, 1991), 316; John Gans, *White House Warriors: How the National Security Council Transformed the American Way of War* (New York: Norton, 2019), 108-109.

18. Atkinson, *Crusade*, 113-114.

19. *Conduct of the Persian Gulf War*, 314, 329.

20. Robert M. Citino, *Blitzkrieg to Desert Storm: The Evolution of Operational Warfare* (Lawrence: University Press of Kansas, 2004), 280.

21. Schwarzkopf, *It Doesn't Take a Hero*, 381.

22. Edward N. Luttwak, *Strategy: The Logic of War and Peace*, rev. ed. (Cambridge, MA: Harvard University Press, 2001), 113-117.

23. Coram, *Boyd*, 355.

24. Stephen Robinson, *The Blind Strategist: John Boyd and the American Art of War* (Dunedin, NZ: Exisle, 2021), 249–253; Michael Evans, *The Continental School of Strategy: The Past, Present and Future of Land Power* (Duntroon ACT, Australia: Land Warfare Studies Centre, 2004), 54.

25. Citino, *Blitzkrieg to Desert Storm*, 289–290.

26. Freedman and Karsh, *Gulf Conflict*, 95.

27. Richard N. Haass, *War of Necessity, War of Choice: A Memoir of Two Iraq Wars* (New York: Simon and Schuster, 2009), 103.

28. Bush and Scowcroft, *World Transformed*, 454.

29. Schwarzkopf, *It Doesn't Take a Hero*, 462.

30. Quoted in Michael R. Gordon, "The Last War Syndrome: How the United States and Iraq Learned the Wrong Lessons from Desert Storm," in *Into the Desert: Reflections on the Gulf War*, ed. Jeffrey A. Engel (New York: Oxford University Press, 2013), 128–129.

31. George H. W. Bush, "Address before a Joint Session of Congress," September 11, 1990, University of Virginia, Miller Center, https://millercenter.org/the-presidency/presidential-speeches/september-11-1990-address-joint-session-congress.

32. Patricia A. Weitsman, *Waging War: Alliances, Coalitions, and Institutions of Interstate Violence* (Stanford, CA: Stanford University Press, 2014), 69.

33. Sir Peter de la Billière interview, PBS Frontline Oral History, PBS, https://www.pbs.org/wgbh/pages/frontline/gulf/oral/billiere/1.html.

34. In October 1991, US intelligence officials estimated that 540,000 Iraqi troops, or 43 divisions, were in the KTO. Sarah E. Kreps, *Coalitions of Convenience: United States Military Interventions After the Cold War* (New York: Oxford University Press, 2011), 58.

35. Schwarzkopf, *It Doesn't Take a Hero*, 382.

36. Shibley Telhami, "The Arab Dimension of Saddam Hussein's Calculations: What We Have Learned from Iraqi Records," in Engel, *Into the Desert*, 168–170.

37. Telhami, "Arab Dimension," 163.

38. Youssef M. Ibrahim, "Mubarak Cites Accords To Help Rescue Kuwait," *New York Times*, January 25, 1991.

39. Schwarzkopf, *It Doesn't Take a Hero*, 388–389.

40. Schwarzkopf, *It Doesn't Take a Hero*, 389, 401–403.

41. John A. Warden III, "Employing Air Power in the Twenty-first Century," in *The Future of Air Power in the Aftermath of the Gulf War*, ed. Richard H. Schultz and Robert L. Pfaltzgraff (Maxwell Air Force Basel, AL: Air University Press, 1992), 57–83.

42. Robert A. Pape, *Bombing to Win: Air Power and Coercion in War* (Ithaca, NY: Cornell University Press, 1996), 221–223, 228–240.

43. Kenneth N. Pollack, *Arabs at War: Military Effectiveness, 1948–1991* (Lincoln: University of Nebraska Press, 2002), 237–241.

44. Pape, *Bombing to Win*, 240–245.

45. Powell, *My American Journey*, 511–512.
46. Bush and Scowcroft, *World Transformed*, 452.
47. Atkinson, *Crusade*, chap. 3.
48. Schwarzkopf, *It Doesn't Take a Hero*, 418.
49. Cheney, *In My Time*, 215.
50. Additionally, the United States refused to give Israel the deconfliction codes that would have allowed them to identify friend from foe in the skies over Iraq. This refusal added risk to any contemplated Israeli air mission. Jeremy Pressman, *Warring Friends: Alliance Restraint in International Politics* (Ithaca, NY: Cornell University Press, 2008), 112.
51. Kevin M. Woods, *The Mother of All Battles: Saddam Hussein's Strategic Plan for the Persian Gulf War* (Annapolis, MD: Naval Institute Press, 2008), ch. 2.
52. Lawrence Freedman, *Command: The Politics of Military Operations from Korea to Ukraine* (New York: Oxford University Press, 2022), 265–269.
53. Gordon, "Last War Syndrome," 128.
54. Schwarzkopf, *It Doesn't Take a Hero*, 427.
55. Daryl G. Press, "The Myth of Air Power in the Persian Gulf War and the Future of Warfare," *International Security* 26, no. 2 (Fall 2001): 12n22.
56. *Operation Desert Storm: Evaluation of the Air Campaign*, NSIAD-97-134 (Washington, DC: United States General Accounting Office, June 1997), 147–148.
57. Press, "Myth of Air Power," 28–29.
58. Mikhail Gorbachev, *Memoirs* (New York: Doubleday, 1996), 564.
59. Anatoly S. Chernyaev, *My Six Years with Gorbachev*, ed. Robert English and Elizabeth Tucker (University Park: Penn State Press, 2000), 335.
60. Bush memcon with Soviet Chief of Staff Gen. Mikhail Moiseyev, Washington, DC, October 2, 1990, National Security Archive, https://nsarchive.gwu.edu/document/24320-bush-memcon-soviet-chief-staff-gen-mikhail-moiseyev-washington-d-c-october-2-1990.
61. William Taubman, *Gorbachev: His Life and Times* (New York: Norton, 2017), 574–587.
62. Jeffrey A. Engel, *When the World Seemed New: George H. W. Bush and the End of the Cold War* (New York: Houghton Mifflin Harcourt), 426.
63. James A. Baker III with Thomas M. DeFrank, *The Politics of Diplomacy: Revolution, War, and Peace, 1989–1992* (New York: Putnam, 1995), 402–404.
64. Message to Sir Charles Powell from General Brent Scowcroft, February 19, 1991, National Security Archive, https://nsarchive.gwu.edu/document/21063-1991-02-19-scowcroft-letter.
65. Bush and Scowcroft, *World Transformed*, 471.
66. Baker, *Politics of Diplomacy*, 406.
67. Powell, *My American Journey*, 513–514.
68. Bush and Scowcroft, *World Transformed*, 472.
69. Schwarzkopf, *It Doesn't Take a Hero*, 441–442.
70. Powell, *My American Journey*, 515. Schwarzkopf's recounting of this exchange is similar.

71. Powell, *My American Journey*, 516.
72. Chernyaev, *My Six Years with Gorbachev*, 331–332.
73. Telcon with President Mikhail Gorbachev of the USSR, February 22, 1991, National Security Archive, https://nsarchive.gwu.edu/document/21067-1991-02-22-gorbachev-baker-bush.
74. Bush and Scowcroft, *World Transformed*, 454.
75. Brig. Gen. Robert H. Scales Jr., *Certain Victory: The U.S. Army in the Gulf War* (Washington, DC: Brassey's 1994), 128–133.
76. Gordon, "Last War Syndrome," 131–132.
77. Gordon, "Last War Syndrome," 132.
78. Gordon and Trainor, *Generals' War*, 416.
79. Samuel Helfont, *Iraq against the World: Saddam, America, and the Post–Cold War Order* (New York: Oxford University Press, 2023), 55–56.
80. Powell, *My American Journey*, 521.
81. David Rothkopf, *Running the World: The Inside Story of the National Security Council and the Architects of American Power* (New York: PublicAffairs, 2005), 299.
82. Powell, *My American Journey*, 523.
83. Haass, *War of Necessity, War of Choice*, 130.
84. Patrick E. Tyler, "After the War; Schwarzkopf Says Truce Enabled Iraqis to Escape," *New York Times*, March 27, 1991.
85. Bartholomew Sparrow, *The Strategist: Brent Scowcroft and the Call of National Security* (New York: PublicAffairs, 2015), 416.
86. Gordon and Trainor, *Generals' War*, 429.
87. Schwarzkopf, *It Doesn't Take a Hero*, 488–489.
88. Sparrow, *Strategist*, 417.
89. Thomas R. Pickering, "President George H. W. Bush and the United Nations," in *Transforming Our World: President George H. W. Bush and American Foreign Policy*, ed. Andrew S. Natsios and Andrew H. Card Jr. (New York: Rowman & Littlefield, 2020), 172.
90. Thomas Pickering interview, July 21, 2006, Foreign Affairs Oral History Project, the Association for Diplomatic Studies and Training (hereafter FAOHP).
91. Spencer D. Bakich, *Success and Failure in Limited War: Information and Strategy in the Korean, Vietnam, Persian Gulf, and Iraq Wars* (Chicago: University of Chicago Press, 2014), 179–182.
92. Haass, *War of Necessity, War of Choice*, 136.
93. Pickering interview, FAOHP.
94. Schwarzkopf, *It Doesn't Take a Hero*, 480.
95. Sparrow, *Strategist*, 417–418.

CHAPTER 5. WAR AND STATECRAFT IN THE POST–COLD WAR ERA

1. Michael R. Gordon and General Bernard E. Trainor, *The Generals' War: The Inside Story of the Conflict in the Gulf* (New York: Little, Brown, 1995), 456.

2. George H. W. Bush, "Remarks to Raytheon Missile Systems Plant Employees in Andover, Massachusetts," February 15, 1991, George H. W. Bush Presidential Library & Museum, https://bush41library.tamu.edu/archives/public-papers/2711.

3. Micha Zenko, *Between Threats and War: U.S. Discrete Military Operations in the Post-Cold War World* (Stanford, CA: Stanford University Press, 2016), 30–35.

4. Boutros Boutros-Ghali, "An Agenda for Peace: Preventive Diplomacy, Peacemaking and Peace-Keeping" (New York: UN Department of Public Information, 1992), available at https://digitallibrary.un.org/record/145749?ln=en.

5. Paul Kennedy, *The Parliament of Man: The Past, Present, and Future of the United Nations* (New York: Vintage 2006), 66–67.

6. Richard N. Haass, "The Gulf War: Its Place in History," in *Into the Desert: Reflections on the Gulf War*, ed. Jeffrey A. Engel (New York: Oxford University Press, 2013), 76.

7. Spencer D. Bakich, "The Reluctant Grand Strategist at War: Diplomacy and Force in Bosnia and Kosovo," in *42: Inside the Presidency of Bill Clinton*, ed. Michael Nelson, Barbara A. Perry, and Russell L. Riley (Ithaca, NY: Cornell University Press, 2016), 194.

8. Lawrence Freedman, "The International Politics of the Gulf War," in Engel, *Into the Desert*, 106.

9. Christian Alfonsi, *Circle in the Sand: Why We Went Back to Iraq* (New York: Doubleday, 2006), 173–174.

10. UN Security Council Resolution 687 (1991), United Nations, https://www.un.org/depts/unmovic/documents/687.pdf.

11. Samuel Helfont, *Iraq against the World: Saddam, America, and the Post-Cold War Order* (New York: Oxford University Press, 2023), 64–67.

12. Helfont, *Iraq against the World*, 68–69.

13. George H. W. Bush, "Address before a Joint Session of the Congress on the Persian Gulf Crisis and the Federal Budget Deficit," September 11, 1990, George H. W. Bush Presidential Library & Museum, https://bush41library.tamu.edu/archives/public-papers/2217.

14. National Security Strategy of the United States, August 1991, National Security Archive, https://nssarchive.us/national-security-strategy-1991/.

15. Sergey Radchenko, "Mikhail Gorbachev: The Anatomy of New Thinking," in *Before and After the Fall: World Politics and the End of the Cold War*, ed. Nuno P. Monteiro and Fritz Bartel (New York: Cambridge University Press, 2021), 46–48.

16. William Taubman, *Gorbachev: His Life and Times* (New York: Norton, 2017), 580–582.

17. Angela E. Stent, *The Limits of Partnership: U.S.-Russian Relations in the Twenty-First Century* (Princeton, NJ: Princeton University Press, 2014), 2–5.

18. George H. W. Bush, "Remarks at Texas A&M University in College Station, Texas," December 15, 1992, University of Virginia, Miller Center, https://millercenter.org/the-presidency/presidential-speeches/december-15-1992-remarks-texas-am-university.

19. Patrick E. Tyler, "U.S. Strategy Plan Calls for Insuring No Rivals Develop," *New York Times*, March 8, 1992.

20. Derek Chollet and James Goldgeier, *America between the Wars, from 11/9 to 9/11: The Misunderstood Years between the Fall of the Berlin Wall and the Start of the War on Terror* (New York: PublicAffairs, 2008), 44–46.

21. James Mann, *Rise of the Vulcans: The History of Bush's War Cabinet* (New York: Viking, 2004), 209–213.

22. Melvyn P. Leffler, *Safeguarding Democratic Capitalism: U.S. Foreign Policy and National Security, 1920–2015* (Princeton, NJ: Princeton University Press, 2017), 261–264.

23. Chollet and Goldgeier, *America between the Wars*, 43–52; National Security Strategy of the United States 1993, January 1993, National Security Archive, https://nssarchive.us/wp-content/uploads/2020/04/1993.pdf.

24. Bartholomew Sparrow, *The Strategist: Brent Scowcroft and the Call of National Security* (New York: PublicAffairs, 2015), 485–486.

25. Hal Brands, *Grand Strategy in the Age of Trump* (Washington, DC: Brookings Institution Press, 2018), chap. 1.

26. Rebecca Lissner, *Wars of Revelation: The Transformative Effects of Military Intervention on Grand Strategy* (New York: Oxford University Press, 2022), 147–148.

27. James D. Boys, *Clinton's Grand Strategy: US Foreign Policy in a Post–Cold War World* (London: Bloomsbury, 2015), 55–58.

28. Colin Dueck, *Reluctant Crusaders: Power, Culture, and Change in American Grand Strategy* (Princeton, NJ: Princeton University Press, 2006), 132.

29. Hal Brands and Patrick Porter, "Why Grand Strategy Still Matters in a World of Chaos," *National Interest*, December 10, 2015, https://nationalinterest.org/feature/why-grand-strategy-still-matters-world-chaos-14568.

BIBLIOGRAPHIC ESSAY

Essential treatments of the Persian Gulf War include Lawrence Freedman and Efraim Karsh, *The Gulf Conflict, 1990–1991: Diplomacy and War in the New World Order* (Princeton, NJ: Princeton University Press, 1993); Michael R. Gordon and General Bernard E. Trainor, *The Generals' War: The Inside Story of Conflict in the Gulf* (New York: Little, Brown, 1995); Bob Woodward, *The Commanders* (New York: Touchstone, 1991); Rick Atkinson, *Crusade: The Untold Story of the Persian Gulf War* (New York: Houghton Mifflin, 1993); Steve A. Yetiv, *Explaining Foreign Policy: U.S. Decision Making and the Persian Gulf War*, 2nd ed. (Baltimore: Johns Hopkins University Press, 2004); and Christian Alfonsi, *Circle in the Sand: Why We Went Back to Iraq* (New York: Doubleday, 2006). Two excellent review articles by Robert Divine address the state of the Persian Gulf War literature in the first ten years after the conflict: Robert A. Divine, "Review: Historians and the Gulf War: A Critique," *Diplomatic History* 19, no. 1 (Winter 1995): 117–134 and Robert A. Divine, "The Persian Gulf War Revisited: Tactical Victory, Strategic Failure," *Diplomatic History* 24, no. 1 (Winter 2000): 129–138. Joshua Rovner, "Delusion of Defeat: The United States and Iraq, 1990–1998," *Journal of Strategic Studies* 17, no. 4 (June 2014): 482–507 makes the case that the Gulf War was a strategic victory for the United States. Jeffrey A. Engel, ed., *Into the Desert: Reflections on the Gulf War* (New York: Oxford University Press, 2013) is an excellent source for the most up-to-date scholarship on the various aspects of the war.

Scholarship into Iraqi motivations for and conduct of the war is growing rapidly. Important contributions include Kevin M. Woods, *The Mother of All Battles: Saddam Hussein's Strategic Plan for the Persian Gulf War* (Annapolis, MD: Naval Institute Press, 2008); Kevin M. Woods, David D. Palkki, and Mark E. Stout, eds., *The Saddam Tapes: The Inner Workings of a Tyrant's Regime, 1978–2001* (New York: Cambridge University Press, 2011); and Samuel Helfont, *Iraq against the World: Saddam, America, and the Post-Cold War Order* (New York: Oxford University Press, 2023).

Many books, articles, and reports deal with the military strategic and operational aspects of the war. Two key US government publications are the five volumes and summary report in Eliot A. Cohen, *Gulf War Air Power Survey* (Washington, DC: US Government Printing Office, 1993) and US Department of Defense, *Conduct of the Persian Gulf War: Final Report to Congress* (Washington, DC: US Government Printing Office, 1992). The role of air power is a contested aspect of the war. Key titles include Robert A. Pape, *Bombing to Win: Air Power and Coercion in War* (Ithaca, NY: Cornell University Press, 1996); John Warden, "Employing Air Power in the Twenty-First Century," in *The Future of Air Power in the Aftermath of the Gulf War*, ed. Richard H. Schultz and Robert L. Pfalzgraff Jr. (Maxwell Air Force Base, AL: Air University Press, 1992), 57–82; Daryl G. Press, "The Myth of Air Power in the Persian Gulf War and the Future of Warfare," *International Security* 36, no. 2 (Fall 2001), 5–44; Frederick W. Kagan, *Finding the Target: The Transformation of American Military Policy* (New York: Encounter Books, 2006); Stephen Biddle, "Victory Misunderstood: What the Gulf War Tells Us about the Future of Conflict," *International Security* 21, no. 2 (Fall 1996): 139–179; and Stephen Biddle, *Military Power: Explaining Victory and Defeat in Modern Battle* (Princeton, NJ: Princeton University Press, 2004). For discussions of American land power doctrine, see Robert M. Citino, *Blitzkrieg to Desert Storm: The Evolution of Operational Warfare* (Lawrence, KS: University Press of Kansas, 2004) and Stephen Robinson, *Blind Strategist: John Boyd and the American Art of War* (Dunedin, NZ: Exisle, 2021).

Works situating the Persian Gulf War in the context of American foreign relations toward the Middle East are Lawrence Freedman, *A Choice of Enemies: America Confronts the Middle East* (New York: PublicAffairs, 2008); Steve A. Yetiv, *The Absence of Grand Strategy: The United States in the Persian Gulf, 1972–2005* (Baltimore: Johns Hopkins University Press, 2008); Geoffrey Wawro, *Quicksand: America's Pursuit of Power in the Middle East* (New York: Penguin Press, 2010); and Marc J. O'Reilly, *Unexceptional: America's Empire in the Persian Gulf, 1941–2007* (Lanham, MD: Lexington Books, 2008). Studies that situate the war in the context of the broader sweep of American foreign policy include Hal Brands, *Making the Unipolar Moment: U.S. Foreign Policy and the Rise of the Post-Cold War Order* (Ithaca, NY: Cornell University Press, 2016); Hal Brands,

From Berlin to Baghdad: America's Search for Purpose in the Post-Cold War World (Lexington: University Press of Kentucky, 2008); Stephen Sestanovich, *Maximalist: America in the World from Truman to Obama* (New York: Vintage, 2014); and Derek Chollet and James Goldgeier, *America between the Wars: From 11/9 to 9/11: The Misunderstood Years between the Fall of the Berlin Wall and the Start of the War on Terror* (New York: PublicAffairs, 2008). Kristina Spohr, *Post Wall, Post Square: How Bush, Gorbachev, and Deng Shaped the World after 1989* (New Haven: Yale University Press, 2019) is a magisterial work of international history that contextualizes the Gulf War in the years of rapid systemic transformation. It should be read alongside the impressive Philip Zelikow and Condoleezza Rice, *To Build a Better World: Choices to End the Cold War and Create a Global Commonwealth* (New York: Twelve, 2019).

In addition to broader histories that include the Persian Gulf War, scholars have grappled with several discrete aspects of the conflict. For example, some have argued that the personal diplomacy of President George H. W. Bush was key to the building of the international coalition. Andrew S. Natsios and Andrew H. Card Jr., eds., *Transforming Our World: President George H. W. Bush and American Foreign Policy* (Lanham, MD: Rowman & Littlefield, 2020) offers a range of valuable essays on Bush's foreign policy. With respect to Bush's leadership, see Jeffrey A. Engel, *When the World Seemed New: George H. W. Bush and the End of the Cold War* (New York: Houghton Mifflin Harcourt, 2017); Jon Meacham, *Destiny and Power: The American Odyssey of George Herbert Walker Bush* (New York: Random House, 2015); and Derek Chollet, *The Middle Way: How Three Presidents Shaped America's Role in the World* (New York: Oxford University Press, 2021). Bush's relationships with his two most important advisers are discussed in Bartholomew Sparrow, *The Strategist: Brent Scowcroft and the Call of National Security* (New York: PublicAffairs, 2015) and Peter Baker and Susan Glasser, *The Man Who Ran Washington: The Life and Times of James A. Baker III* (New York: Doubleday, 2020).

Multilateral diplomacy through the United Nations was critical to American strategy. Important works on the topic include Andrew Bennett, Joseph Lepgold, and Danny Unger, eds., *Friends in Need: Burden Sharing in the Persian Gulf War* (London: St. Martin's Press, 1997); Alexander Thompson, *Channels of Power: The UN Security Council and U.S. Statecraft in Iraq* (Ithaca, NY: Cornell University Press, 2009); and David A. Lake, *Entangling Relations: American Foreign Policy in Its Century* (Ithaca, NY: Cornell University Press, 1999). For treatments of wartime civil-military relations, see Dale R. Herspring, *The Pentagon and the Presidency: Civil-Military Relations from FDR to George W. Bush* (Lawrence: University Press of Kansas, 2005); Eliot A. Cohen, *Supreme Command: Soldiers, Statesmen and Leadership in Wartime* (New York: Anchor, 2003); Michael C. Desch, *Civilian Control of the Military: The Changing Security Environment* (Baltimore: Johns Hopkins University Press, 1999); Richard K. Betts, *American Force: Dangers, Delusions, and Dilemmas in National Security* (New York: Columbia University Press, 2013); and Thomas E. Ricks, *The Generals: American Military Command from World War II to Today* (New York: Penguin, 2013).

There is strong scholarly consensus that the foreign policy process in the George H. W. Bush administration was particularly, if not uniquely, effective. See Spencer D. Bakich, *Success and Failure in Limited War: Information and Strategy in the Korean, Vietnam, Persian Gulf, and Iraq Wars* (Chicago: University of Chicago Press, 2014); Bartholomew Sparrow, "Organizing Security: How the Bush Presidency Made Decisions on War and Peace," in *41: Inside the Presidency of George H. W. Bush*, ed. Michael Nelson and Barbara Perry (Ithaca, NY: Cornell University Press, 2014), 81–99; Ivo H. Daalder and I. M. Destler, *In the Shadow of the Oval Office: Profiles of the National Security Advisers and the Presidents They Served—From JFK to George W. Bush* (New York: Simon & Schuster, 2011); and David Rothkopf, *Running the World: The Inside Story of the National Security Council and the Architects of American Power* (New York: PublicAffairs, 2006). James Mann, *The Rise of the Vulcans: The History of Bush's War Cabinet* (New York: Viking, 2004) provides background on the relationships among the officials in Bush's administration, while James Mann, *The Great Rift: Dick Cheney, Colin Powell, and the Broken Friendship That Defined an Era* (New York: Henry Holt, 2020) examines the relationship between Cheney and Powell.

On the meaning of the new world order, see Engel, *When the World Seemed New*; Sparrow, *The Strategist*; Brands, *From Berlin to Baghdad*;

Brands, *Making the Unipolar Moment*; and Rosemary Hollis, "The U.S. Role: Helpful or Harmful?" in *Iran, Iraq, and the Legacies of War*, ed. Lawrence G. Potter and Gary G. Sick (New York: Palgrave Macmillan, 2004), 193–211. Rebecca Lissner, *Wars of Revelation: The Transformative Effects of Military Intervention on Grand Strategy* (New York: Oxford University Press, 2022) argues that the Gulf War paved the way for American hegemony in the post–Cold War era by revealing the extent of America's preponderance of power.

Memoirs of key actors in the Persian Gulf War are plentiful and should be thoroughly consulted. First among these is George Bush and Brent Scowcroft, *A World Transformed* (New York: Knopf, 1998). For Bush's diaries and letters, see George H. W. Bush, *All the Best: My Life in Letters and Other Writings* (New York: Scribner, 2013) and Jeffrey A. Engel, ed., *The China Diary of George H. W. Bush: The Making of a Global President* (Princeton, NJ: Princeton University Press, 2008). Memoirs from other top officials in the George H. W. Bush administration include James A. Baker III with Thomas M. DeFrank, *The Politics of Diplomacy: Revolution, War, and Peace, 1989–1992* (New York: Putnam, 1995); Dick Cheney with Elizabeth Cheney, *In My Time: A Personal and Political Memoir* (New York: Threshold Editions, 2011); Colin Powell with Joseph E. Persico, *My American Journey* (New York: Random House, 1995); H. Norman Schwarzkopf with Peter Petre, *It Doesn't Take a Hero: The Autobiography of General H. Norman Schwarzkopf* (New York: Bantam Books, 1992); Robert M. Gates, *From the Shadows: The Ultimate Insider's Story of Five Presidents and How They Won the Cold War* (New York: Simon & Schuster, 2007); Richard N. Haass, *War of Necessity, War of Choice* (New York: Simon and Schuster, 2009); and Dennis Ross, *The Missing Piece: The Inside Story of the Fight for the Middle East Peace* (New York: Ballantine, 1996).

The following oral history collections are particularly valuable: Miller Center, University of Virginia, "The George H. W. Bush Oral History," Presidential Oral History Project (https://millercenter.org/the-presidency/presidential-oral-histories/george-h-w-bush); "Frontline Diplomacy: The Foreign Affairs Oral History Collection of the Association for Diplomatic Studies and Training," Library of Congress (https://www.loc

.gov/collections/foreign-affairs-oral-history); and PBS, *Frontline*, "The Gulf War: An Oral History," (https://www.pbs.org/wgbh/pages/frontline/gulf/oral).

For archival holdings, the George H. W. Bush Presidential Library and Museum at Texas A&M University in College Station, TX is indispensable. President Bush's Public Papers are searchable online at https://bush41library.tamu.edu/archives/public-papers. The Digital National Security Archive, a component of the National Security Archive at George Washington University in Washington, DC, offers many important collections, including "Iraqgate: Saddam Hussein, U.S. Policy and the Prelude to the Persian Gulf War, 1980–1994," (http://proquest.libguides.com/dnsa/iraqgate). Also available through the National Security Archive are three excellent electronic briefing books: William Burr and Jeffrey T. Richelson, eds., "Operation Desert Storm: Ten Years Later," National Security Archive Electronic Briefing Book no. 39 (January 17, 2001) (https://nsarchive2.gwu.edu/NSAEBB/NSAEBB39/); Jeffrey Richelson, ed., "Iraq and Weapons of Mass Destruction," National Security Archive Electronic Briefing Book no. 80 (February 11, 2004), (https://nsarchive2.gwu.edu/NSAEBB/NSAEBB80/index.htm); and Joyce Battle, ed., "Saddam Hussein Talks to the FBI: Twenty Interviews and Five Conversations with 'High Value Detainee # 1' in 2004," National Security Archive Electronic Briefing Book no. 279 (July 1, 2009) (https://nsarchive2.gwu.edu/NSAEBB/NSAEBB279/index.htm).

INDEX

Achille Lauro incident, 16
Ahmad, Hasheem, 101
Ahmad al-Sabah, Jaber al-, 73
Ahtisaari, Martii, 107
Allen, Richard, 16
Andropov, Yuri, 17
Arab nationalism, 67
Assertive Multilateralism, 113
Aziz, Tariq, 56, 80–81, 95–96

Baker, James
  Bush partnership with, 21
  characteristics of as secretary of state, 21
  coalition of states and, 2
  on coercive diplomacy, 65–66
  Conventional Forces in Europe (CFE) treaty and, 45
  in Core Group (Big 8), 27
  German unification role of, 39–46
  Kuwait invasion and, 57, 59, 60–61
  leadership of, 16, 37, 111
  on Malta summit, 123n48
  meeting with Qian Qichen, 76
  on the Middle East peace process, 49–50
  New Atlanticism of, 37
  Operation Desert Shield and, 74
  Operation Desert Storm and, 84, 95, 98, 103
  pre-war meeting with Tariq Aziz, 80–81
  as problem-solver, 22
  Richard Cheney and, 53
  sanctions viewpoint of, 74
  Security Council Resolution 678 meeting of, 77–79
  staffers of, 24
  US-Soviet relations and, 48–49
Baker, Peter, 22

Baltic states, 110
Barak, Ehud, 91–92
Bessmertnykh, Alexander, 95–96
Billière, Peter de la, 89
Bipartisan Accord on Central America, 49–50
Boomer, Walter, 96, 99
Bosnia, 4, 106
Boutros-Ghali, Boutros, 106
Boyd, John, 87
Brezhnev, Leonid, 17
Brezhnev Doctrine, 36
Bush, George H. W.
  as ambassador to the United Nations, 10–11, 12, 14
  characteristics of, 11, 15
  coalition of states and, 2
  as conservative, 15
  in crisis management committee, 16
  as Director of Central Intelligence (DCI), 15
  diplomacy style of, 11, 12, 14, 17, 46–47, 113–114
  empathy of, 18
  foreign policy decision-making process of, 20–30
  grand strategic vision of, 29–30
  influences on American grand strategy, 5–6
  as internationalist, 19, 113–114
  liberalism of, 20
  in National Security Planning group, 16
  operational code of, 119n32
  personal writings of, 13–14, 17, 97
  political roles of, 10
  pragmatism of, 20
  relationship engagements by, 11
  Republican National Committee (RNC) leadership of, 11–12

Bush, George H. W. (*cont.*)
   Senate election defeat of, 10
   strategic beliefs of, 7–8, 18–20, 52–53
   travels of, 17
   United Nations and, 11
   as vice president, 15–16
   view of changing international system, 31

cabinet government, characteristics of, 16
Carver, George, 15
Central America, Bipartisan Accord on Central America and, 49–50
Central Intelligence Agency (CIA), 15
Chamberlain, Neville, 59
Cheney, Richard
   American primacy and, 111
   Colin Powell and, 23–24
   in Core Group (Big 8), 27
   Kuwait invasion and, 59
   Operation Desert Shield and, 73
   Operation Desert Storm and, 84, 85, 86, 91, 96, 103
   as outlier in Bush administration, 23
   personal relationships of, 21
   staffers of, 24
   strategic viewpoints of, 53, 114
   as unilateralist, 23
   worldview of, 22–23
Chernenko, Konstantin, 17
Chernyaev, Anatoly, 41, 62, 70, 94
China, 12–13, 14, 17, 47–48, 69, 76, 79
Citino, Robert, 87
Clinton, Bill, 113
coalition building, 65–71
coercive diplomacy, 65–71
Cold War, 6, 32–33, 115
Commonwealth of Independent States, 110
Conference on Security and Cooperation in Europe (CSCE), 44–45, 52
Conventional Forces in Europe (CFE) proposal, 41

Conventional Forces in Europe (CFE) treaty, 45
Core Group (Big 8), 27
crisis management committee, 16
Cuba, 79
Cultural Revolution, 12
Czechoslovakia, 44

Deaver, Michael, 16
Defense Planning Guidance (DPG), 111–112
defense program (United States), 64
Deng Xiaoping, 47
Department of Defense (DOD), 52–53, 111, 112
deputies' access to principals, norm regarding, 27–28
Deputies Committee (DC), 26, 27, 28
disease in post-war Iraq, 107–108
domino theory, 14
due process, norm regarding, 28

Eagleburger, Lawrence, 57–58, 92
economy (United States), budget compromise in, 66
Egypt, 89
Engel, Jeffrey, 46
Europe, as whole and free, 31–41. *See also specific locations*

Fahd bin Abdulaziz Al Saud (king of Saudi Arabia), 87
Faisal, Saud al-, 72
Federal Republic of Germany (FRG), 33, 40
Ford, Gerald, 12
foreign policy
   decision-making process regarding, 20–30, 114–115
   deputies' access to principals' norm in, 27–28
   due process norm in, 28
   information flow pattern regarding, 29
   liberalism in, 20

norms regarding, 27–28
proportion in, 19
quality control norm in, 28
strategic discipline regarding, 19
France, 67–68, 86
Freeman, Chas, 74
Fukuyama, Francis, 35

Gates, Robert, 26, 27, 28, 75–76
German Democratic Republic (GDR), 33, 35, 38, 40
Germany
   NATO and, 35–36, 37–38, 39–40, 42–46, 63
   "not one inch" formulation with, 43
   Soviet Union and, 42–46
   unification, 21, 33–41, 42, 45, 48, 51, 63, 124n66
   US grand strategy regarding, 33, 34–35, 37–38, 39–41
Glaspie, April, 56
Glasser, Susan, 22
global political alliance, 66
Goldwater-Nichols reforms, 24
Gorbachev, Mikhail
   Bush's meetings with, 17, 41–42, 43, 52–53, 109
   coalition building with, 70
   coup against, 110
   diplomacy attempts of, 94, 95–96, 98
   economic challenges and, 109–110
   election of, 45
   financial support to, 44
   frustrations of, 31–32
   Kuwait invasion and, 62
   limitations of, 43
   "New Thinking" of, 109
   new world order conception of, 94
   Operation Desert Storm response of, 94, 95–96, 98
   "the pause" and, 32
   pressures on, 37, 95
   relations with, 1
   Ronald Reagan and, 31
   Security Council resolution meeting of, 77–79
   war resolution and, 76–77
Gordon, Michael, 99
grand strategy, 5–6, 114. *See also* New World Order grand strategy
Gulf War. *See* Persian Gulf War

Haass, Richard, 57, 67, 88
Haig, Al, 16
Helsinki Final Act, 42–43, 45
Highway of Death, 99–100, 103
Hitler, Adolf, 59, 73, 113
Holl Lute, Jane, 25–26
humanitarian disasters, 7, 113
Hungary, 34, 44
Hussein, Saddam
   Adolf Hitler parallels with, 73
   Arab nationalism and, 67
   Baker's assessment of, 78
   Bush's remarks regarding, 105
   characteristics of, 5, 59, 105
   invasion of Kuwait by, 1, 55, 56–65, 70–71
   Mikhail Gorbachev and, 109
   post-war actions of, 87
   pre-war challenges of, 1
   sanctions on, 73, 74
   as threat, 4
   UN-imposed obligations on, 68
   US objectives regarding, 5
   US removal plans regarding, 108
   victory theory of, 93
   war preparation by, 56
   war reactions of, 91, 92–93
   withdrawal agreement of, 96
   world view of, 1–2
Hussein bin Talal (king of Jordan), 56

International Atomic Energy Agency, 4
Iran-Contra scandal, 25–26
Iran-Iraq War, 1
Iraq
   casualties of, 100
   devastation in, 107–108

Iraq (cont.)
    economic ties to, 67–68
    financial challenges of, 1
    invasion by, 1, 55, 56–65, 70–71
    military operations against, 110
    no-fly zone over, 106
    Operation Desert Storm effects on, 2–3
    Operation Provide Comfort and, 106
    Republican Guard of, 3
    sanctions on, 73, 74, 108
    troop statistics of, 72
    UN Security Council resolution 687 and, 107
    war effects on, 94
    war preparation by, 56
    war strategies of, 91
    withdrawal of, 99–100, 101
Iraqi Republican Guard (IRG), 85, 86, 91, 99, 101
Israel, 91, 92, 131n50

Japan, 4
Jeremiah, David, 85
Johnson, Bob, 97

Kennedy, Paul, 68
Khafji, Saudi Arabia, 93
Kimmitt, Robert, 57
Kissinger, Henry, 13–14, 22, 49, 65
Kohl, Helmut, 38, 39, 40–41, 43, 44
Kosovo, 4
Kravchuk, Leonid, 110
Kurds, 4, 102, 105–106
Kuwait
    containment plan regarding, 72, 73
    invasion of, 1, 55, 56–65, 70–71
    objectives regarding, 5
    oil field fires in, 96
    Operation Desert Storm and, 3
    tin cup diplomacy and, 66
    withdrawal from, 99–100, 101
    See also Operation Desert Shield; Operation Desert Storm

Kuwaiti Theater of Operations (KTO), 2–3

Lilley, James, 69

MacArthur, Douglas, 85
Malta summit, 41–42, 123n48
Martel, William, 50
McCaffery, Barry, 99
Meese, Edwin, 16
Middle Kingdom Syndrome, 12–13
Mitterrand, Francois, 76–77
modern system of warfare style, 3
Moiseyev, Mikhail, 94
Mubarak, Hosni, 56, 70, 89

national security, decision-making regarding, 16
national security advisor, role and characteristics of, 16, 24, 26
National Security Council (NSC), 27
National Security Directive (NSD), 1, 23, 26–27, 36–37, 45, 46, 60, 62–63
National Security Planning group, 16
National Security Strategy, 109, 112
New Atlanticism, 37
New World Order grand strategy
    challenges of, 7
    China and, 47–48
    Cold War and, 115
    collective action and, 64–65
    collective security and rule of law in, 108–109
    commonwealth for freedom and, 65
    Europe whole and free and, 31–41
    Germany and, 33, 34–35, 37–38, 39–41
    Kuwait invasion and, 61–62
    managing threats to America's objectives and, 46–54
    objectives of, 60, 62–63
    opportunities from, 113

INDEX 145

origin of, 32, 113–115
overview of, 6, 31, 50–54
Soviet Union as beyond
   containment in, 41–46
strategies and, 46–54
tactics and, 46–54
United Nations and, 63–64, 67, 69
New York Times (newspaper), 10, 111
Nicaragua, 49
Nixon, Richard, 10, 11–12
Nixon administration, dysfunction
   of, 25
Noriega, Manuel, 27, 50
North Atlantic Treaty Organization
   (NATO), 35–36, 37–38, 39–40,
   42–46, 63

oil industry, threats to, 55
101st Airborne Division, 99
Operation Desert Shield
   air component of, 82–83
   casualties of, 3
   coalition for, 71
   grand strategy and, 6
   objectives of, 72
   overview of, 2, 61
   resources for, 82
   statistics regarding, 72, 76
Operation Desert Storm
   air war of, 90
   Arab state involvement in, 89–90
   casualties of, 3
   cease-fire and, 101
   congressional vote regarding, 81
   decision for, 72–81
   failures of, 102–103
   grand strategy and, 6
   ground attack in, 84, 90–99
   Instant Thunder of, 90
   "the left hook" regarding, 3, 86
   maximum destruction principle
   of, 88
   no-fly zone and, 102–103
   origin of, 2–3, 82–90

   overview of, 103–104
   plans regarding, 84–86
   statistics regarding, 82, 94
   UN Security Council resolutions
   and, 88
   war termination of, 99–103
Operation Just Cause, 50
Operation Provide Comfort, 106

Panama, 50
Panama Canal Zone, 50
Panama Defense Force (PDF), 50
"the pause," 32
Peay, J. H. Binford, III, 99
Persian Gulf War
   aftermath of, 7, 105
   influences to, 116
   New World Order grand strategy
   and, 6
   objectives of, 5, 115
   outcome of, 4, 112–113
   overview of, 3–4
   reasons for, 113
   See also Operation Desert Shield;
   Operation Desert Storm
Pickering, Thomas, 57, 68–69, 70, 81,
   102, 103
Poland, 34, 44
policy coordinating committees
   (PCCs), 26
Powell, Colin
   containment viewpoint of, 73
   in Core Group (Big 8), 27
   leadership of, 23
   Operation Desert Shield and, 73
   Operation Desert Storm and, 83, 84,
   85–86, 91–92, 96, 97–98, 100
   reputation of, 74
   war termination and, 107
   war viewpoint of, 74–75
President's Foreign Intelligence
   Advisory Board (PFIAB), 15
Primakov, Yevgeny, 44, 77, 95
Principals Committee (PC), 26–27

Qian Qichen, 76
quality control, norm regarding, 28
Quayle, Dan, 27

Radchenko, Sergey, 109
Reagan, Ronald, 15–16, 17, 31
Reagan administration, disorganization of, 25
Regional Defense Strategy, 112
Republican National Committee (RNC), 11–12
resolution for war, conditions of, 76
Rovner, Joshua, 4–5
Rowen, Henry, 85

Safwan, 107
Saigon, 14, 19
sanctions, 73, 74, 108
Saudi Arabia
    culture of, 71
    Kuwait invasion and, 57
    Operation Desert Shield and, 2
    Operation Desert Storm and, 86
    tin cup diplomacy and, 66, 67
    US troops in, 71, 74
Schwarzkopf, H. Norman, 71, 74–75, 82–85, 87–88, 92, 96–98, 100–101, 103, 104
Scowcroft, Brent
    on coalition building, 66
    communication by, 29
    in Core Group (Big 8), 27
    Iran-Contra scandal and, 25–26
    Kuwait invasion and, 57, 59, 60
    leadership of, 110–111, 114
    as national security advisor, 14, 24–25
    Operation Desert Shield and, 73, 92
    Operation Desert Storm and, 84–85, 100, 103
    overview of, 24–25
    personal relationships of, 21
    Principals Committee (PC) and, 26–27
    quality control and, 28
    as realist, 25
    Richard Cheney and, 53
    strategic perspective of, 22
secretary of state, role of, 60–61
Shamir, Yitzhak, 92
Shevardnadze, Eduard, 31, 61, 77–79, 95
Shi'a, 4, 101, 102, 106
Shultz, George, 16
Shushkevich, Stanislav, 110
shuttle diplomacy, 49
Smith, Tony, 65
sovereignty, 5, 11, 33, 60, 67, 69, 96, 101, 106, 108
Soviet Union
    as beyond containment, 41–46
    China and, 48
    Cold War and, 6
    collapse of, 116
    conventional force reductions by, 122n28
    Conventional Forces in Europe (CFE) proposal and, 41
    economic challenges of, 109–110
    financial support to, 44
    foreign policy of, 41–42
    German Democratic Republic (GDR) and, 33, 38
    German unification and, 42–46
    Iraq's relations with, 1
    Kuwait invasion and, 61
    Operation Desert Storm viewpoint of, 94
    "the pause" and, 32
    troop reduction of, 41
    United States' relations with, 6, 12, 36–37, 42, 48–49, 63, 78, 114
    views on confronting Saddam Hussein, 78–79
    World War II and, 4
    zero-zero option and, 17
Sparrow, Bartholomew, 25
Spohr, Kristina, 34
Sultan, Khalid bin, 90

Sununu, John, 27
Syria, 90

Thatcher, Margaret, 57
Tiananmen massacre, 48
tin cup diplomacy, 66
Tower, John, 22
Tower Commission, 25–26
Trans-Pacific Partnership, with China, 47–48
Turkey, 105–6
Twenty-Fourth Mechanized Division, 99
"Two Plus Four Power" formula, 40, 42, 51, 68

UN Charter, article 51 of, 77
United Kingdom, 66, 86
United Nations, 4, 20, 63–64, 67, 69, 113
United States Central Command (CENTCOM), 71, 72, 82, 84–85, 86, 88, 89
UN Security Council
  coalition building and, 68
  limitations from, 101–102

resolution 660, 57
resolution 661 of, 69
resolution 678 of, 69, 79
resolution 687 of, 103, 107
resolution 688 of, 105–106
resolution voting by, 69
US VII Corps, 99
US XVIII Corps, 99

Warden, John III, 82, 90
Washington Star (newspaper), 10
Weinberger, Caspar, 16
Weitsman, Patricia, 71
Wilsonianism, 65
Wolfowitz, Paul, 72–73, 91
World War II, outcome of, 4

Yeltsin, Boris, 110
Yemen, 79
Yugoslavia, 106

Zelikow, Philip, 24, 28, 66
zero-zero option, 17
Zoellick, Robert, 43

www.ingramcontent.com/pod-product-compliance
Lightning Source LLC
Chambersburg PA
CBHW030219170426
43194CB00007BA/793